Easy Cake Cookbook

Easy CAKE *Cookbook*

75
SINFULLY SIMPLE RECIPES
FOR BAKE-AND-EAT CAKES

MIRANDA COUSE

Photography by Annabelle Breakey

ROCKRIDGE
PRESS

For general information on our other products and services or to obtain technical support, please contact our Customer Care Department within the U.S. at (866) 744-2665, or outside the U.S. at (510) 253-0500.

Rockridge Press publishes its books in a variety of electronic and print formats. Some content that appears in print may not be available in electronic books, and vice versa.

TRADEMARKS: Rockridge Press and the Rockridge Press logo are trademarks or registered trademarks of Callisto Media Inc. and/or its affiliates, in the United States and other countries, and may not be used without written permission. All other trademarks are the property of their respective owners. Rockridge Press is not associated with any product or vendor mentioned in this book.

Interior and Cover Designer: Julie Schrader
Photo Art Director: Michael Hardgrove
Editor: Pam Kingsley
Production Editor: Ashley Polikoff
Photography © 2019 Annabelle Breakey
Food Styling by Elisabet der Nederlanden

ISBN: Print 978-1-64152-952-5 |
eBook 978-1-64152-953-2
R0

To my husband, Wesley, and son, Lucian, for always being my cake testers and biggest fans.

Contents

Strawberry Cream Cheese
Coffee Cake, page 12

Introduction

In 2013, I was a stay-at-home mom busy getting to know my new son and a new town, since my husband had accepted a job that required us to move to a place where I knew no one. Cooped up in my house, I became restless and decided I needed to take up a hobby, something that could provide me with an outlet for my creativity while also making me a part of a greater community. That's when my website, Cookie Dough and Oven Mitt, came to be.

I am a self-taught baker. So, when I started my website, I knew I wanted to focus on sharing *easy* recipes. I always envisioned fellow moms searching for a simple homemade cake recipe that they could whip up for their family.

What I didn't know when I started Cookie Dough and Oven Mitt was that I would fall in love with developing recipes. I've always loved baking, but recipe developing took my passion to a whole new level—I enjoy learning about the science of baking and often feel like a mad scientist throwing baking ingredients into a bowl to see what happens.

But take it from me and a lesson I learned the hard way: You can't just toss ingredients together into a bowl and call it a cake. My first from-scratch cake recipe for the blog was a bit of a train wreck. Through trial and error, I discovered that cakes require more than a little guesswork to become light, airy, sweet treats. That first cake was sunken in the middle but, at the same time, managed to spill over the edge of the cake pan, resulting in a burned mess on the floor of my oven that took forever to clean.

That burned disaster didn't stop me from baking cakes, however. Instead, I schooled myself on the science behind cake making and the factors that needed to align to yield a perfectly moist, tender cake. Sometimes it's still a learning process. But, after years of creating recipes, I can tell you that there's no better feeling than making a cake from scratch and having it come out perfect. I still do a little victory dance every time that happens. And, if you're like me, this book will give you plenty of reasons to dance.

This book offers up simple, scrumptious recipes for cake lovers big on taste but short on time. These are mix-and-bake recipes that don't need frostings or icings to be delicious (but I offer some recipes in chapter 7 just in case you want to gild the lily, and I also suggest optional ways to finish each cake in a feature called Top It Off). No matter the occasion or season, or whether you just need a grab-and-go cake bar, are craving a sweet coffee cake, or want to try your hand at a rustic-yet-simple skillet cake, the just-perfect recipe is here for you.

Don't worry, my fellow self-taught baker—I'll walk you through all of this step-by-step, including the best pans to use and how to prep them. So throw on your apron, dig the ingredients out of your pantry, and start baking some cakes. If you enjoy the recipes, don't forget to share the book with your friends and family.

Happy baking!
Miranda

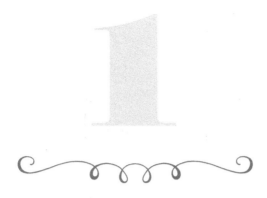

YOUR GUIDE TO CAKE-BAKING SUCCESS

Baking the perfect cake doesn't need to be difficult. But it does take time and a little basic baking knowledge. To make cake making more approachable, this chapter covers the perfect pans to use, how to prep for a recipe, and even the best tools to use. I will also go into detail about measuring and mixing ingredients. Before you know it, you'll be baking your way through this book with ease. I hope you find some family favorites along the way.

HAVE THE RIGHT PANS

There are a handful of specific baking pans that every home baker should keep in her arsenal. The following pans will be needed for the recipes in this book.

BUNDT PAN

The classic 10-inch (12-cup) Bundt pan is essential for the Bundt Cake chapter. I recommend using a nonstick pan because Bundt cakes have a tendency to stick even when you coat the pans with baking spray. If using a Bundt pan with a design in it, keep in mind that the more grooves the pan has, the harder it is to get the spray evenly distributed inside and the more likely it is that the cake will stick. If you use a pan smaller than 12 cups, the batter will likely overfill the pan.

LOAF PAN

The loaf pan I prefer is 8½ by 4½ inches and made from aluminized steel. A glass pan of the same size will work, too. The 9-by-5-inch pan is another common size loaf pan that can be used. If you're using the larger pan, the bake times may be shorter than what's noted in the recipes and the cakes will be thinner. You can easily check for doneness by inserting a toothpick to the center of the cake. When it comes out clean, it's done. I would start doing this 10 minutes earlier than the recipe indicates.

BAKING PANS

For snacking cakes that don't call for a loaf pan, an 8-inch square pan can be used. It makes the perfect-size squares for snacking. A 9-inch square pan can also be used, but your cake won't bake up as high and will be done quicker.

A lot of my coffee cake recipes call for a 9-by-13-inch aluminum or glass pan. These pans can be interchanged without affecting the bake time. The 9-by-13-inch pan is one of the most common baking pans, which is why I include this size for some of the cakes.

SKILLET

The skillet cakes were tested in a 10-inch cast iron skillet. There are many different sizes of skillet pans, so be prepared to keep an eye on your cake if you're using something other than a 10-inch skillet. If it's smaller, the bake time will be longer; if it's bigger, the bake time will be shorter.

RAMEKINS, SMALL PANS, AND BAKING SHEETS

I use ramekins for the Little Cakes chapter, which is mostly single-serving cakes. There are so many different ramekin sizes and shapes, as well as other individual portion pans like mini Bundt pans and mini springform pans. I opted to bake in 6-ounce round ramekins. The different shapes won't matter as long as they have a 6-ounce capacity. If you're using smaller ramekins, don't overfill them. The cake will spill out.

If you're using individual-portion pans such as mini Bundt pans, mini springform pans, or a large coffee cup, be sure that they will hold ¾ cup of batter. This will ensure that the baking time is the same as the recipe instructions.

Use a baking pan of any size to set your ramekins on to prevent any spilling in the oven. Unlike a sheet pan, a baking pan always has raised edges.

6-INCH ROUND PAN

The Yellow Cake for Two recipe on page 115 calls for a 6-inch round cake pan. I chose an aluminum pan. To ensure that the cake comes out easily, coat the pan with nonstick baking spray and place a 6-inch round piece of parchment paper in the bottom of the pan.

PROPER PAN PREP

One of the most important steps in each cake recipe is prepping the pan properly. Each recipe will describe this in detail. In some cases, such as for Bundt cakes, a nonstick baking spray with flour is used; Baker's Joy is a popular and widely available brand. A substitution for the nonstick baking spray with flour is to generously grease the pan and dust it with flour. Tap out any excess flour into the trash.

Other pan prepping involves first lining pans with parchment paper or aluminum foil and then coating it with a nonstick baking spray. The purpose of lining a pan is for easy removal of the cake, like the snack cakes.

While the oven is preheating, take this time to prep the pans. It's a great habit to get into so there is never any waiting time once the batter is ready. Having the pan and batter ready for the oven at the same time keeps the air pockets that help the cake batter rise from deflating.

TOOLS TO HAVE ON HAND

There are a few basic tools and appliances you should have on hand to make cake baking a lot easier:

DRY MEASURING CUPS: These are for measuring dry ingredients, such as flour and sugar. Try to have a set with 1-cup, ¾-cup, ½-cup, ⅓-cup, and ¼-cup measuring cups. I use all of these measurements in this book.

SET OF MEASURING SPOONS: This is a must. You should always use measuring spoons for the leavening agents, such as baking soda and baking powder.

LIQUID MEASURING CUP: I use a 2-cup measuring cup for the liquids.

MICROPLANE: Several recipes in the book require grated citrus zest, and using a microplane instead of a box grater makes this task so much easier. Only zest until the white pith starts to show. Then rotate the citrus and start zesting in another spot until all that's left is pith.

MINI FOOD PROCESSOR: This comes in handy to chop nuts, as well as to purée fruit to add to the batter, such as strawberries. It also works great for finely chopping cookies.

ELECTRIC MIXER: You can certainly mix up batter by hand, but an electric mixer (whether a stand mixer or handheld electric mixer) makes it a lot easier and faster. It also helps create the perfect air pockets when creaming butter and sugar together. An electric mixer with three speeds will work perfectly.

WOODEN SPOON: If you don't have a mixer, a wooden spoon can be used instead. It will take longer to incorporate the ingredients and to build the air pockets needed to help the cakes rise, but this old-fashioned tool has stood the test of time.

SPATULA: Both a rubber or silicone spatula will work. A spatula is used to scrape the sides and bottoms of bowls, measuring cups, and the beaters. It's also the tool of choice to fold in ingredients and spread the batter out.

ASSEMBLE AND PREP YOUR INGREDIENTS

First, read your recipe. What kind of pan do you need? How should it be prepped—line it with parchment paper or aluminum foil, grease and dust it with flour, or just coat the pan with non-stick baking spray? What ingredients do you need? Pull them from the pantry and refrigerator, then assemble them near your workstation.

Most recipes, unless it is specifically stated otherwise, call for butter and/or cream cheese that should be at room temperature before mixing in. You'll need to allow about 30 minutes for that. Some recipes require ingredient prep work, such as chopping and/or toasting nuts or draining fruit, such as canned pineapple or maraschino cherries. Allow about 10 minutes for this.

And don't forget to preheat the oven!

Easy Hacks to Warm Up Butter or Cream Cheese

Many of my recipes call for the butter and/or cream cheese to be at room temperature, which takes about 30 minutes if it's coming straight out of the refrigerator. You'll know it's ready when you can easily press your finger into it but it still feels cool. Using butter and cream cheese at this temperature ensures a smooth batter with no lumps.

But if you're in a hurry, here are three ways to speed up the process:

1. Cut the butter or cream cheese into small chunks. This exposes more surface area, allowing it to warm up faster.
2. Microwave the butter or cream cheese in 5-second intervals on a plate, flipping it as you microwave it each time, until it softens sufficiently.
3. This method only works for butter, but it works especially well for frozen butter: Grate it using the biggest holes of a box grater. Once you're done, the butter will soften in minutes.

MINDFUL MEASURING

Liquid ingredients should always be measured in a liquid or graduated measuring cup. Always hold it at eye level, and use the measurement mark to make sure the liquid measurement is accurate.

These cake recipes are forgiving, so I use dry measuring cups for the dry ingredients instead of weighing them with a kitchen scale.

To measure flour, I "fluff" the flour by scooping it into the cup several times and pouring it back out before scooping the flour for the recipe. This is the first step to preventing the flour from being packed into the cup. Once the flour is scooped, use the back side of a butter knife to level the flour without packing it into the cup.

Because of its softness, brown sugar should be tightly packed into a dry measuring cup for accurate measurement, packed all the way up and leveled straight across the top of the cup. The sugar will come out of the measuring cup in one big piece; just break it apart with a wooden spoon.

Softening Hard Brown Sugar

We've all been there—you pull the box of brown sugar out to discover it is rock hard. No worries, here's an easy save: Place it in a microwave-safe bowl and lay a damp paper towel over it. Microwave for about 20 seconds. That should soften it up nicely.

MIX IT RIGHT

Did you know mixing ingredients out of order can affect how the cake turns out? It does. In the case of my Decadent Chocolate Bundt Cake (page 36), if the dry ingredients are added to the wet instead of the other way around, lumps of flour will form that are almost impossible to get rid of without overmixing the batter.

Also, undermixing or overmixing ingredients can also affect the cake. If the butter and sugar aren't mixed long enough to form air pockets, the final crumb of the cake won't be light and tender. And, if the eggs are overmixed, the cake can end up dry and very dense.

If you follow the recipe directions, you'll be fine. Here are some of the mixing methods you may come across and how to do them.

MIX JUST UNTIL COMBINED

This means mix the batter just until the flour disappears and you can no longer see any traces of flour in the batter. If you continue to mix beyond this point, you will develop the gluten in the flour, which will result in a gummy, dense cake.

CREAM THE BUTTER AND SUGAR TOGETHER

You can do this by hand with a wooden spoon, but you will have a better result with an electric mixer. The butter should be at room temperature. Beat the butter and sugar together until the mixture is light and fluffy, which can take 1 to 3 minutes. Doing this beats air into the mixture, creating air pockets that will yield a lighter-textured cake and a finer crumb.

FOLD INTO THE BATTER

When you fold, you are carefully combining two mixtures or two ingredients without stirring or beating them. If you are folding in liquid or dry ingredients, use a spatula. If you are folding in whipped cream or whipped egg whites, use a wire whisk.

For example, to fold whipped cream into chocolate ganache, add the whipped cream to a bowl of cooled ganache. Run the spatula or whisk along the bottom of the bowl to bring the ganache up over the top of the whipped cream. Repeat this motion until everything is evenly distributed and you have a light, airy chocolate whipped cream.

BAKE IT RIGHT

Proper oven temperature and keeping an eye on the time are both very important in baking cakes. A too-high temperature can result in an overdone top and a raw-batter center. A too-low temperature can result in a longer bake time, a darker color, and a flat cake due to the leavening having a slower rise.

Losing track of the time and overbaking a cake can happen in minutes. It can turn a soft, moist cake into a hard, dry cake. Be mindful when you check the cake; opening the oven door too often to check on it will let the heat out and affect the cake's texture, as well.

THE IMPORTANCE OF PREHEATING

I recommend preheating the oven as part of your prep work. Let it sit at the required temperature for 15 minutes before beginning to bake. This will allow all of the surfaces inside the oven to come up to the correct temperature, which will allow for even baking and help prevent the heat from escaping when opening the oven to put the pan of batter inside. Failure to preheat the oven can result in a heavy, undercooked cake.

To accurately preheat the oven, use an in-oven thermometer. This is also ideal if you have been noticing your cakes aren't baking according to the time given in the recipe. It's an indication that your oven calibration is possibly incorrect.

To calibrate the oven, preheat the oven with the in-oven thermometer inside. Keep an eye on the thermometer. It will let you know if the heat needs to be higher or lower, but only adjust it after you've waited a significant amount of time to ensure that the temperature is no longer rising. I recommend waiting 15 to 20 minutes before adjusting the oven temperature.

After the adjustments are made, keep an eye on the oven thermometer to make sure the temperature has been corrected. This means another 10 to 20 minutes of watching and waiting. In the end, all these adjustments for the correct temperature are worth it. The cake comes out perfectly.

RECOGNIZING DONENESS

Over the years, I've come to realize it's important to be able to recognize when your baked goods are done. This means it's best to use the time given in recipes as a guideline. For cakes, you should start paying close attention 10 minutes before the bake time stated in the recipe. The cakes will be golden brown on top and will spring back when gently pressed down near the center. If the indentation doesn't spring back, the cake isn't done and needs to bake longer.

Another quick and easy way to check the cake's doneness is to poke the center of the cake with a toothpick. If the cake is done, the toothpick will have moist crumbs on it or may be completely clean. If the toothpick has batter on it, leave the cake in to bake a bit longer.

Trust Your Nose

Always trust your nose when baking. If you think, "Wow, that smells so good," get up right away to check on the cake. Chances are it's done or very close to being done.

COOL IT! OR NOT

The cooling times for cakes can vary. Some cakes, like Bundt cakes, should be left to cool for only about 10 minutes before being turned out onto a wire rack; otherwise, the cake will stick to the pan. More delicate cakes need to be left in the pan to cool completely. And some cakes need to be rolled up while they're still hot.

The cakes in this book tend to need only 10 minutes to cool before removing them. This allows the cakes to release from the pan, create less crumb, and to firm up.

When removing a cake from its pan, turn it over onto a wire rack to cool completely. The wire rack is ideal because it's slightly raised off the counter to allow air to circulate underneath as well as on top of the cake.

S'mores Coffee Cake, page 30

COFFEE CAKES

Who can resist cake for breakfast? Coffee cake is the perfect pick-me-up when it's served with a hot cup of coffee. Each cake has a crumb topping for sweetness and extra crunch. The coffee cakes in this chapter range from a classic cinnamon coffee cake to a unique coffee cake with a chocolate crumb, as well as plenty of fruity coffee cakes. And, while perfectly delectable on their own, if you want some extra zing, they are amazing topped with a glaze from chapter 7 (see page 123).

STRAWBERRY CREAM CHEESE COFFEE CAKE

This is the ultimate breakfast cake. It has a layer of cake, cream cheese, fresh strawberries, and a delicious crumb topping.

PREP TIME: 20 MINUTES • BAKE TIME: 60 MINUTES • YIELD: 12 SERVINGS

FOR THE CRUMB TOPPING

1½ cups all-purpose flour

½ cup (1 stick) unsalted butter, at room temperature

½ cup granulated sugar

½ cup packed light brown sugar

¼ teaspoon salt

FOR THE STRAWBERRY LAYER

1½ cups strawberries, hulled and diced

2 tablespoons granulated sugar

2 teaspoons cornstarch

1. Preheat the oven to 350°F. Spray a 9-by-13-inch baking pan with nonstick baking spray. Set aside.

2. For the topping, in a medium bowl, using an electric mixer on medium speed, beat the flour, butter, granulated and brown sugars, and salt together until the butter is well incorporated and the topping looks like wet sand. Set aside.

3. For the strawberry layer, in a small bowl, toss the strawberries, sugar, and cornstarch together until the sugar and cornstarch are well distributed and have dissolved. Set aside.

4. For the cream cheese layer, in a medium bowl, using the mixer on medium speed, beat the cream cheese and sugar together until creamy. Beat in the vanilla, then the egg. Scrape down the sides and bottom of the bowl and beat in any remaining bits on medium speed. Set aside.

5. For the cake, in a large bowl, using the mixer on medium speed, beat the melted butter, sugar, sour cream, and vanilla together until the sour cream is combined. Add the egg and beat until worked into the batter. Scrape down the sides and bottom of the bowl.

FOR THE CREAM CHEESE LAYER

1 (8-ounce) package full-fat cream cheese, at room temperature

½ cup granulated sugar

1 teaspoon vanilla extract

1 large egg

FOR THE CAKE

½ cup (1 stick) unsalted butter, melted

¾ cup granulated sugar

½ cup full-fat sour cream

1 teaspoon vanilla extract

1 large egg

1½ cups all-purpose flour

1 teaspoon baking powder

¼ teaspoon salt

6. In a small bowl, stir together the flour, baking powder, and salt. Add the dry ingredients to the butter-sugar mixture in the large bowl and beat on medium speed, just until the flour is worked into the batter.

7. Spread the batter into the prepared baking pan with a spatula. Spoon dollops of the cream cheese layer on top of the batter. Using a spatula, lightly spread the cream cheese out as much as possible without disturbing the batter. Spoon the strawberry layer on top of the cream cheese layer. Sprinkle the crumb topping on top of the strawberries, evenly distributing it over the entire cake. Bake until a toothpick inserted into the center comes out clean, 55 to 60 minutes.

8. Let the cake cool completely before serving. Cut into three strips lengthwise, then four strips widthwise, for 12 servings.

STORAGE: Will keep tightly wrapped with plastic wrap or foil or in an airtight container in the refrigerator up to 3 to 4 days.

VARIATION: Replace the diced strawberries with 1½ cups diced, pitted cherries.

TOP IT OFF: Dust the cake with powdered sugar.

ORANGE COFFEE CAKE

This fun and tangy coffee cake is made with fresh orange juice and zest and the crumb topping has orange zest for an added pop of flavor. It's a tender cake that goes great with a cup of coffee.

PREP TIME: 15 MINUTES • BAKE TIME: 50 MINUTES • YIELD: 12 SERVINGS

FOR THE CRUMB TOPPING

1 cup all-purpose flour

½ cup (1 stick) unsalted butter, at room temperature

½ cup granulated sugar

½ cup packed light brown sugar

1 tablespoon grated orange zest

¼ teaspoon salt

FOR THE CAKE

1¼ cups (2½ sticks) unsalted butter, melted

1 cup granulated sugar

½ cup full-fat sour cream

1 tablespoon grated orange zest

1. Preheat the oven to 350°F. Spray a 9-by-13-inch baking pan with nonstick baking spray. Set aside.

2. For the topping, in a medium bowl, using an electric mixer on medium speed, beat the flour, butter, granulated and brown sugars, orange zest, and salt together until the butter is well incorporated and the topping looks like wet sand. Set aside.

3. For the cake, in a large bowl, using the mixer on medium speed, beat the melted butter, sugar, sour cream, orange zest, and vanilla together until well combined. Add the eggs and beat until worked into the batter. Scrape down the sides and bottom of the bowl.

4. In a medium bowl, stir together the flour, baking powder, and salt. Add the dry ingredients and orange juice to the large bowl in multiple additions, alternating back and forth between the two, starting and ending with the flour mixture and beating on medium speed. Scrape down the sides and bottom of the bowl and stir in any unmixed bits of batter with a spatula.

1 teaspoon
vanilla extract

2 large eggs

3 cups all-purpose flour

1 tablespoon
baking powder

½ teaspoon salt

¾ cup pulp-free
orange juice

5. Spread the batter into the prepared baking pan with a spatula. Sprinkle the crumb topping on top of the batter, evenly distributing it. Bake until a toothpick inserted into the center comes out clean, 44 to 50 minutes.

6. Let the cake cool completely before serving. Cut into three strips lengthwise, then four strips widthwise, for 12 servings.

STORAGE: Will keep tightly wrapped with plastic wrap or foil or in an airtight container at room temperature for 4 to 5 days.

TOP IT OFF: If you want even more orange flavor, drizzle with Orange Glaze (see page 128).

BLUEBERRY BUCKLE

Sweet and a little bit tart, this is the perfect cake to take to a summer picnic or a family get-together.

PREP TIME: 15 MINUTES • BAKE TIME: 60 MINUTES • YIELD: 12 SERVINGS

FOR THE CRUMB TOPPING

1 cup all-purpose flour

½ cup (1 stick) unsalted butter, at room temperature

½ cup granulated sugar

½ cup packed light brown sugar

1 teaspoon ground cinnamon

¼ teaspoon salt

FOR THE CAKE

1½ cups granulated sugar

1¼ cups vegetable oil

¾ cup full-fat sour cream

2 teaspoons vanilla extract

2 large eggs

3 cups all-purpose flour

1. Preheat the oven to 350°F. Spray a 9-by-13-inch baking pan with nonstick baking spray. Set aside.

2. For the crumb topping, in a medium bowl, using an electric mixer on medium speed, beat the flour, butter, granulated and brown sugars, cinnamon, and salt together until the butter is well incorporated and the topping looks like wet sand. Set aside.

3. For the cake, in a large bowl, using the mixer on medium speed, beat the sugar, oil, sour cream, and vanilla together until well combined. Add the eggs and beat until they are worked into the batter. Scrape down the sides and bottom of the bowl.

4. In a medium bowl, stir together the flour, baking powder, and salt. Add the dry ingredients and buttermilk to the large bowl in multiple additions, alternating back and forth between the two, starting and ending with the flour mixture and beating on medium speed. Scrape down the sides and bottom of the bowl and stir in any unmixed bits of batter with a spatula. Fold the blueberries into the batter until evenly distributed.

5. Spread the batter into the prepared baking pan with a spatula. Sprinkle the crumb topping on top of the batter, evenly distributing it.

1 tablespoon
baking powder

½ teaspoon salt

½ cup buttermilk

1½ cups fresh or
frozen blueberries

6. Bake until a toothpick inserted into the center comes out clean, 55 to 60 minutes.

7. Let cool completely before serving. Cut into three strips lengthwise, then four strips widthwise, for 12 servings.

STORAGE: Will keep tightly wrapped with plastic wrap or foil or in an airtight container at room temperature for 4 to 5 days.

VARIATION: Add the grated zest of 1 lemon and 1 teaspoon lemon extract to the cake batter for a blueberry-lemon buckle.

CINNAMON COFFEE CAKE

This classic is a go-to recipe for me. It has a signature cinnamon-sugar strip in the middle of the cake and is topped with a cinnamon crumb. It's out of this world with a cup of hot coffee.

PREP TIME: 15 MINUTES • BAKE TIME: 50 MINUTES • YIELD: 12 SERVINGS

FOR THE CRUMB TOPPING

1 cup all-purpose flour

½ cup (1 stick) unsalted butter, at room temperature

½ cup granulated sugar

½ cup packed light brown sugar

1 teaspoon ground cinnamon

¼ teaspoon salt

FOR THE CAKE

1½ cups granulated sugar

1¼ cups (2½ sticks) unsalted butter, at room temperature

2 teaspoons vanilla extract

2 large eggs

3 cups all-purpose flour

1. Preheat the oven to 350°F. Spray a 9-by-13-inch baking pan with nonstick baking spray. Set aside.

2. For the topping, in a medium bowl, using an electric mixer on medium speed, beat the flour, butter, granulated and brown sugars, cinnamon, and salt together until the butter is well incorporated and the topping looks like wet sand. Set aside.

3. For the cake, in a large bowl, using the mixer on medium speed, cream the sugar, butter, and vanilla together until light and fluffy. Add the eggs and beat until they are worked into the batter. Scrape down the sides and bottom of the bowl.

4. In a medium bowl, stir together the flour, baking powder, and salt. Add the dry ingredients and buttermilk to the butter-sugar mixture in the large bowl in multiple additions, alternating back and forth between the two, starting and ending with the flour mixture and beating on medium speed. Scrape down the sides and bottom of the bowl with a spatula and stir in any unmixed bits of batter.

5. In a small bowl, combine the brown sugar and cinnamon.

1 tablespoon
baking powder

½ teaspoon salt

1 cup buttermilk

**FOR THE
CINNAMON SUGAR**

½ cup packed light
brown sugar

1½ teaspoons
ground cinnamon

6. Spread half the batter into the prepared baking pan with a spatula. Sprinkle the cinnamon sugar on top of the batter, evenly distributing it. Add the rest of the batter on top of the cinnamon-sugar layer. Use a spatula to spread out the batter. Sprinkle the crumb topping on top of the batter, evenly distributing it. Bake until a toothpick inserted into the center comes out clean, 45 to 50 minutes.

7. Let the cake cool completely before serving. Cut into three strips lengthwise, then four strips width-wise, for 12 servings.

STORAGE: Will keep tightly wrapped with plastic wrap or foil or in an airtight container at room temperature for 4 to 5 days.

TOP IT OFF: For additional pizzazz, dust the top of the cake with powdered sugar before serving.

MAPLE-PECAN COFFEE CAKE

This coffee cake reminds me of fall. It tastes like maple syrup with a pecan and cinnamon-sugar layer in the middle. The nutty flavor is boosted by the pecans in the crumb topping.

PREP TIME: 15 MINUTES • BAKE TIME: 57 MINUTES • YIELD: 12 SERVINGS

FOR THE CRUMB TOPPING

1 cup all-purpose flour

½ cup (1 stick) unsalted butter, at room temperature

½ cup granulated sugar

½ cup packed light brown sugar

1 teaspoon ground cinnamon

¼ teaspoon salt

1 cup chopped pecans

FOR THE CAKE

1¼ cups (2½ sticks) unsalted butter, room temperature

1 cup granulated sugar

½ cup maple syrup

1 teaspoon vanilla extract

1 teaspoon maple extract

2 large eggs

1. Preheat the oven to 350°F. Coat a 9-by-13-inch baking pan with nonstick baking spray. Set aside.

2. For the crumb topping, in a medium bowl, using an electric mixer on medium speed, beat the flour, butter, granulated and brown sugars, cinnamon, and salt together until the butter is well incorporated and the topping looks like wet sand. Stir in the pecans. Set aside.

3. For the cake, in a large bowl, using the mixer on medium speed, beat the butter, sugar, maple syrup, vanilla, and maple extract together until well combined. Add the eggs and beat until they are worked into the batter. Scrape down the sides and bottom of the bowl.

4. In a medium bowl, stir together the flour, baking powder, and salt. Add the dry ingredients and buttermilk to the butter-sugar mixture in the large bowl in multiple additions, alternating back and forth between the two, starting and ending with the flour mixture and beating on medium speed. Scrape down the sides and bottom of the bowl and stir in any unmixed bits of batter with a spatula.

5. In a small bowl, combine the brown sugar, cinnamon, and pecans.

3 cups all-purpose flour

1 tablespoon
baking powder

½ teaspoon salt

½ cup buttermilk

**FOR THE PECAN
CINNAMON SUGAR**

½ cup packed light
brown sugar

1½ teaspoons
ground cinnamon

½ cup chopped pecans

6. Spread half the batter in the prepared baking pan with a spatula. Sprinkle the pecan cinnamon sugar on top of the batter, evenly distributing it. Add the rest of the batter on top of pecan cinnamon sugar layer. Use a spatula to spread out the batter. Sprinkle the crumb topping on top of the batter, evenly distributing it. Bake until a toothpick inserted into the center comes out clean, 52 to 57 minutes.

7. Let the cake cool completely before serving. Cut into three strips lengthwise, then four strips widthwise, for 12 servings.

STORAGE: Will keep tightly wrapped with plastic wrap or foil or in an airtight container at room temperature for 4 to 5 days.

VARIATION: Substitute walnuts for the 1 cup pecans in the crumb topping and the ½ cup pecans in the cinnamon sugar mixture to make a maple walnut coffee cake.

SWEET POTATO COFFEE CAKE

I love sweet potatoes with brown sugar and cinnamon on them, which is what inspired this coffee cake. It has a faint orange color from the mashed sweet potatoes. There's a layer of cinnamon sugar in the center of each slice and a cinnamon-sugar crumb topping.

PREP TIME: 15 MINUTES • BAKE TIME: 49 MINUTES • YIELD: 12 SERVINGS

FOR THE CRUMB TOPPING

1 cup all-purpose flour

½ cup (1 stick) unsalted butter, at room temperature

½ cup granulated sugar

½ cup packed light brown sugar

1 teaspoon ground cinnamon

¼ teaspoon salt

FOR THE CAKE

1½ cups granulated sugar

1 cup mashed cooked sweet potatoes

1 cup vegetable oil

2 teaspoons vanilla extract

2 large eggs

1. Preheat the oven to 350°F. Coat a 9-by-3-inch baking pan with nonstick baking spray. Set aside.

2. For the topping, in a medium bowl, using an electric mixer on medium speed, beat the flour, butter, granulated and brown sugars, cinnamon, and salt together until the butter is well incorporated and the topping looks like wet sand. Set aside.

3. For the cake, in a large bowl, using the mixer on medium speed, beat the granulated sugar, mashed sweet potatoes, oil, and vanilla together until well combined. Add the eggs and beat until they are worked into the batter. Scrape down the sides and bottom of the bowl.

4. In another medium bowl, stir together the flour, baking powder, cinnamon, salt, nutmeg, and ginger. Add the dry ingredients and evaporated milk to the butter–sweet potato mixture in the large bowl in multiple additions, alternating back and forth between the two, starting and ending with the flour mixture and beating on medium speed. Scrape down the sides and bottom of the bowl and stir in any unmixed bits of batter with a spatula.

5. In a small bowl, combine the brown sugar and cinnamon.

2¾ cups
all-purpose flour

1 tablespoon
baking powder

1 teaspoon
ground cinnamon

½ teaspoon salt

½ teaspoon
ground nutmeg

¼ teaspoon
ground ginger

½ cup evaporated milk

FOR THE
CINNAMON SUGAR

½ cup packed light
brown sugar

1½ teaspoons
ground cinnamon

6. Spread half the batter in the prepared baking pan with a spatula. Sprinkle the cinnamon sugar on top of the batter, evenly distributing it. Add the rest of the batter on top of the cinnamon-sugar layer. Use a spatula to spread out the batter. Sprinkle the crumb topping on top of the batter, evenly distributing it. Bake until a toothpick inserted into the center comes out clean, 44 to 49 minutes.

7. Let the cake cool completely before serving. Cut into three strips lengthwise, then four strips width-wise, for 12 servings.

STORAGE: Will keep tightly wrapped with plastic wrap or foil or in an airtight container at room temperature for 4 to 5 days.

TIP: To easily cook a sweet potato, poke it with a fork, place it on a paper towel, and microwave it for 2 to 3 minutes per side. Let the sweet potato cool before peeling and mashing it.

TOP IT OFF: For an extra-decadent finish, top this with miniature marshmallows. Sprinkle a single layer of marsh-mallows on top as soon as the cake is out of the oven.

BANANA COFFEE CAKE

Do you love banana bread? If so, you will love this moist, intense banana-flavored coffee cake. The crumb topping, with its brown sugar and cinnamon combination, makes an amazing addition to the cake.

PREP TIME: 15 MINUTES • BAKE TIME: 55 MINUTES • YIELD: 12 SERVINGS

FOR THE CRUMB TOPPING

1 cup all-purpose flour

½ cup (1 stick) unsalted butter, at room temperature

1 cup packed light brown sugar

1 teaspoon ground cinnamon

¼ teaspoon salt

FOR THE CAKE

1¼ cups (2½ sticks) unsalted butter, melted

1 cup granulated sugar

½ cup packed light brown sugar

1 cup mashed overripe bananas (about 3 bananas)

2 teaspoons vanilla extract

2 large eggs

1. Preheat the oven to 350°F. Coat a 9-by-13-inch baking pan with nonstick baking spray. Set aside.

2. For the crumb topping, in a medium bowl, using an electric mixer on medium speed, beat the flour, butter, brown sugar, cinnamon, and salt together until the butter is well incorporated and the topping looks like wet sand. Set aside.

3. For the cake, in a large bowl, using the mixer on medium speed, beat the butter, granulated and brown sugars, bananas, and vanilla together until well combined. Add the eggs and beat until they are worked into the batter. Scrape down the sides and bottom of the bowl.

4. In another medium bowl, stir together the flour, baking powder, cinnamon, and salt. Add the dry ingredients and buttermilk to the butter-sugar mixture in the large bowl in multiple additions, starting and ending with the flour mixture and beating on medium speed. Scrape down the sides and bottom of the bowl and stir in any unmixed bits of batter with a spatula.

5. In a small bowl, combine the brown sugar and cinnamon.

3 cups all-purpose flour

1 tablespoon
baking powder

½ teaspoon
ground cinnamon

½ teaspoon salt

½ cup buttermilk

**FOR THE
CINNAMON SUGAR**

½ cup packed light
brown sugar

1½ teaspoons
ground cinnamon

6. Spread half the batter in the prepared baking pan with a spatula. Sprinkle the cinnamon sugar on top of the batter, evenly distributing it. Add the rest of the batter on top of the cinnamon sugar. Use a spatula to spread out the batter. Sprinkle the crumb topping on top of the batter, evenly distributing it. Bake until a toothpick inserted into the center comes out clean, 50 to 55 minutes.

7. Let the cake cool completely before serving. Cut into three strips lengthwise, then four strips widthwise, for 12 servings.

STORAGE: Will keep tightly wrapped with plastic wrap or foil or in an airtight container at room temperature for 4 to 5 days.

TIP: To ripen bananas faster, place them in a paper bag and store in a dark area for 1 to 2 days.

CHOCOLATE COFFEE CAKE

This moist chocolate coffee cake is so delicious it will satisfy any chocolate craving. I love that it doesn't require any baking chocolate, just cocoa powder.

PREP TIME: 15 MINUTES • BAKE TIME: 60 MINUTES • YIELD: 12 SERVINGS

FOR THE CRUMB TOPPING

¾ cup all-purpose flour

¾ cup packed light brown sugar

½ cup granulated sugar

½ cup (1 stick) unsalted butter, at room temperature

¼ cup unsweetened cocoa powder

¼ teaspoon salt

FOR THE CAKE

1½ cups granulated sugar

1¼ cups vegetable oil

½ cup full-fat sour cream

2 teaspoons vanilla extract

2 large eggs

2 cups all-purpose flour

1. Preheat the oven to 350°F. Coat a 9-by-13-inch baking pan with nonstick baking spray. Set aside.

2. For the crumb topping, in a medium bowl, using an electric mixer on medium speed, beat the flour, brown and granulated sugars, butter, cocoa, and salt together until the butter is well incorporated and the topping looks like dark, wet sand. Set aside.

3. For the cake, in a large bowl, using the mixer on medium speed, beat the sugar, oil, sour cream, and vanilla together until well combined. Add the eggs and beat until they are worked into the batter. Scrape down the sides and bottom of the bowl.

4. In another medium bowl, stir together the flour, cocoa, baking powder, and salt. Add the dry ingredients and buttermilk to the sugar-oil mixture in the large bowl in multiple additions, alternating back and forth between the two, starting and ending with the flour mixture and beating on medium speed. Scrape down the sides and bottom of the bowl and stir in any unmixed bits of batter with a spatula.

5. Spread the batter into the prepared baking pan with a spatula. Sprinkle the crumb topping on top of the batter, evenly distributing it.

½ cup unsweetened cocoa powder

1 tablespoon baking powder

½ teaspoon salt

¾ cup buttermilk

6. Bake until a toothpick inserted into the center comes out clean, 55 to 60 minutes.

7. Let the cake cool completely before serving. Cut into three strips lengthwise, then four strips widthwise, for 12 servings.

STORAGE: Will keep tightly wrapped with plastic wrap or foil or in an airtight container at room temperature for 4 to 5 days.

TOP IT OFF: If you desire an extra chocolatey coffee cake, sprinkle chocolate chips on top of the crumbs while the cake is still hot. The chips will melt into the crumb topping.

CHOCOLATE CHIP COFFEE CAKE

This is for chocolate chip lovers everywhere. It's satisfying to cut into a cake and see chocolate chips evenly distributed throughout.

PREP TIME: 15 MINUTES • BAKE TIME: 60 MINUTES • YIELD: 12 SERVINGS

FOR THE CRUMB TOPPING

1 cup all-purpose flour

½ cup (1 stick) unsalted butter, at room temperature

½ cup granulated sugar

½ cup packed light brown sugar

¼ teaspoon salt

FOR THE CAKE

1½ cups granulated sugar

1¼ cups vegetable oil

¾ cup full-fat sour cream

2 teaspoons vanilla extract

2 large eggs

3 cups all-purpose flour

1 tablespoon baking powder

½ teaspoon salt

½ cup buttermilk

1½ cups semisweet or milk chocolate chips

1. Preheat the oven to 350°F. Coat a 9-by-13-inch baking pan with nonstick baking spray. Set aside.

2. For the crumb topping, in a medium bowl, using an electric mixer on medium speed, beat the flour, butter, granulated and brown sugars, and salt together until the butter is well incorporated and the topping looks like wet sand. Set aside.

3. For the cake, in a large bowl, using the mixer on medium speed, beat the granulated sugar, oil, sour cream, and vanilla together until well combined. Add the eggs and beat until they are worked into the batter. Scrape down the sides and bottom of the bowl.

4. In another medium bowl, stir together the flour, baking powder, and salt. Add the dry ingredients and buttermilk to the sugar-oil mixture in the large bowl in multiple additions, alternating back and forth between the two, starting and ending with the flour mixture and beating on medium speed. Scrape down the sides and bottom of the bowl and stir in any unmixed bits of batter with a spatula. Fold the chocolate chips into the batter until evenly distributed.

5. Spread the batter in the prepared baking pan with a spatula. Sprinkle the crumb topping on top of the batter, evenly distributing it. Bake until a toothpick inserted into the center comes out clean, 55 to 60 minutes.

6. Let the cake cool completely before serving. Cut into three strips lengthwise, then four strips widthwise, for 12 servings.

STORAGE: Will keep tightly wrapped with plastic wrap or foil or in an airtight container at room temperature for 4 to 5 days.

VARIATION: For an even prettier cake, try adding miniature chocolate chips as well as regular-size chocolate chips.

S'MORES COFFEE CAKE

This s'mores coffee cake is bursting with layers of flavor.
It starts with a graham cracker cake, topped with milk chocolate,
followed by marshmallow creme, with chocolate crumbs
sprinkled on top. It's a family favorite.

PREP TIME: 20 MINUTES • BAKE TIME: 54 MINUTES • YIELD: 12 SERVINGS

**FOR THE
CRUMB TOPPING**

1¼ cups packed light
brown sugar

¾ cup all-purpose flour

½ cup (1 stick)
unsalted butter, at
room temperature

¼ cup unsweetened
cocoa powder

¼ teaspoon salt

FOR THE CAKE

1½ cups
granulated sugar

1¼ cups (2½ sticks)
unsalted butter, melted

1 teaspoon
vanilla extract

2 large eggs

2½ cups
all-purpose flour

1½ cups graham cracker
crumbs (10 whole
graham crackers)

1. Preheat the oven to 350°F. Coat a 9-by-13-inch baking pan with nonstick baking spray. Set aside.

2. For the crumb topping, in a medium bowl, using an electric mixer on medium speed, beat the brown sugar, flour, butter, cocoa, and salt together until the butter is well incorporated and the topping looks like dark, wet sand. Set aside.

3. For the cake, in a large bowl, using the mixer on medium speed, cream the granulated sugar, butter, and vanilla together until light and fluffy. Add the eggs and beat until they are worked into the batter. Scrape down the sides and bottom of the bowl.

4. In another medium bowl, stir together the flour, graham cracker crumbs, baking powder, and salt. Add the dry ingredients and buttermilk to the butter-sugar mixture in the large bowl in multiple additions, alternating back and forth between the two, starting and ending with the flour mixture and beating on medium speed. Scrape down the sides and bottom of the bowl and stir in any unmixed bits of batter with a spatula.

5. Spread the batter in the prepared baking pan with a spatula. Arrange the chocolate bars on top of the batter. Dollop the marshmallow creme on top of the chocolate bars. Use a spatula to carefully spread it in an even layer without moving the candy bars too much. Sprinkle the crumb topping on top of the

1 tablespoon
baking powder

½ teaspoon salt

1 cup buttermilk

7 (1.55-ounce) milk
chocolate bars

1 (7- to 7½-ounce) jar
marshmallow creme

marshmallow creme, evenly distributing it. Bake until a toothpick inserted into the center comes out clean, 49 to 54 minutes.

6. Let the cake cool completely before serving. Cut into three strips lengthwise, then four strips widthwise, for 12 servings.

STORAGE: Will keep tightly wrapped with plastic wrap or foil or in an airtight container at room temperature for 4 to 5 days.

TIP: If the marshmallow creme starts popping through the crumb topping and browning too much, cover the pan with a piece of aluminum foil. Fold it in half to make a tent top so it stands above the cake and doesn't stick.

MILK AND COOKIES COFFEE CAKE

Who doesn't love Oreos, especially in your breakfast coffee cake?
This coffee cake has a layer of them sprinkled in the center of it,
as well as on top. Normally, toppings are optional, but you won't
want to leave off the glaze.

PREP TIME: 20 MINUTES • BAKE TIME: 55 MINUTES • YIELD: 12 SERVINGS

**FOR THE COOKIE
CRUMB TOPPING**

¾ cup all-purpose flour

½ cup (1 stick)
unsalted butter, at
room temperature

½ cup granulated sugar

½ cup packed light
brown sugar

¼ teaspoon salt

10 Oreo cookies, crushed

FOR THE CAKE

1½ cups
granulated sugar

1¼ cups vegetable oil

¾ cup full-fat sour cream

1 teaspoon
vanilla extract

2 large eggs

3 cups all-purpose flour

1 tablespoon
baking powder

1. Preheat the oven to 350°F. Coat a 9-by-13-inch baking pan with nonstick baking spray. Set aside.

2. For the cookie crumb topping, in a medium bowl, using an electric mixer on medium speed, beat the flour, butter, granulated and brown sugars, and salt together until the butter is well incorporated and the topping looks like wet sand. Stir in the crushed Oreos. Set aside.

3. For the cake, in a large bowl, using the mixer on medium speed, beat the sugar, oil, sour cream, and vanilla together until well combined. Add the eggs and beat until they are worked into the batter. Scrape down the sides and bottom of the bowl.

4. In another medium bowl, combine the flour, baking powder, and salt. Add the dry ingredients and buttermilk to the sugar-oil mixture in the large bowl, alternating back and forth between the two, starting and ending with the flour mixture and beating on medium speed. Scrape down the sides and bottom of the bowl and stir in any unmixed bits of batter with a spatula.

5. Spread half the batter in the prepared baking pan with a spatula. Sprinkle the crushed Oreos on top of the batter. Spread the remaining batter over the cookie layer without disturbing the crumbs. Sprinkle

½ teaspoon salt

½ cup buttermilk

1¾ cups crushed Oreo cookies (15 Oreos)

FOR THE GLAZE

1 cup powdered sugar

1½ to 2 tablespoons whole milk

½ teaspoon vanilla extract

the crumb topping on top of the batter, evenly distributing it. Bake until a toothpick inserted into the center comes out clean, 50 to 55 minutes.

6. Let the cake cool completely before serving. While the cake is cooling, make the glaze.

7. For the glaze, in a small bowl, whisk together the powdered sugar, milk, and vanilla. Drizzle the glaze over the cake after it's cooled completely. Cut into three strips lengthwise, then four strips widthwise, for 12 servings.

STORAGE: Will keep tightly wrapped with plastic wrap or foil or in an airtight container at room temperature for 4 to 5 days.

VARIATION: You can substitute 1 cup of any other crushed sandwich cookie for the Oreos.

Decadent Chocolate Bundt Cake, page 36

BUNDT CAKES

The best part about Bundt cakes is that they don't require layers and layers of frosting for the final product to be perfectly smooth. Instead, dust a little powdered sugar on top or stir together a glaze to drizzle on it (check out the glazes in the Toppings chapter, page 123).

All the cakes in this chapter can serve 12 people, or serve 6 people twice! That's totally up to you.

DECADENT CHOCOLATE BUNDT CAKE

This chocolatey Bundt cake is incredibly moist. The milk chocolate ganache layer baked into the top takes this cake just a little over the top.

PREP TIME: 15 MINUTES • BAKE TIME: 60 MINUTES • YIELD: 12 SERVINGS

FOR THE CAKE

1 cup strongly brewed coffee

¾ cup (1½ sticks) unsalted butter, cubed

¾ cup unsweetened cocoa powder

2 tablespoons vegetable oil

1 cup full-fat sour cream

2 teaspoons vanilla extract

2 cups all-purpose flour

1½ cups granulated sugar

1½ teaspoons baking soda

½ teaspoon baking powder

½ teaspoon salt

2 large eggs, lightly beaten

1. Preheat the oven to 325°F. Coat a 10-inch (12-cup) Bundt pan with nonstick baking spray with flour.

2. In a medium microwave-safe bowl, microwave the coffee and butter for 2 to 2½ minutes, until the butter is completely melted. Whisk in the cocoa and oil until smooth. Whisk in the sour cream and vanilla until combined.

3. In a large bowl, combine the flour, sugar, baking soda, baking powder, and salt. Add the cocoa mixture and eggs and whisk together until the batter is smooth. Pour the batter into the prepared Bundt pan.

4. For the ganache, in a small microwave-safe bowl, microwave the chocolate chips and cream in 30-second intervals, stirring after each interval, until the ganache is smooth and creamy. Pour the ganache in the center of the chocolate cake batter all the way around the Bundt pan. Bake until a toothpick inserted into the center comes out clean, 53 to 60 minutes.

FOR THE GANACHE

1 cup milk
chocolate chips

½ cup heavy cream

5. Let cool for about 10 minutes, then turn the cake out onto a wire rack to cool completely. Cut and serve.

STORAGE: Will keep tightly wrapped with plastic wrap or foil or in an airtight container in the refrigerator for 4 to 5 days.

VARIATION: You can vary the flavor of the ganache by substituting bittersweet, semisweet, or white chocolate chips or peanut butter chips for the milk chocolate chips.

VANILLA POUND CAKE

This is a dense and buttery pound cake with the most wonderful vanilla flavor.

PREP: 15 MINUTES • BAKE: 1 HOUR 15 MINUTES • YIELD: 12 SERVINGS

2 cups granulated sugar

1 cup (2 sticks) unsalted butter, at room temperature

1 tablespoon vanilla extract

4 large eggs

2¾ cups all-purpose flour

½ teaspoon baking powder

½ teaspoon baking soda

½ teaspoon salt

1 cup whole milk

1. Preheat the oven to 325°F. Coat a 10-inch (12-cup) Bundt pan with nonstick baking spray with flour.

2. In a large bowl, using an electric mixer on medium speed, cream the sugar and butter together until light and fluffy. Beat in the vanilla, then the eggs one at a time.

3. In a medium bowl, sift together the flour, baking powder, baking soda, and salt. Add the dry ingredients and milk to the butter-sugar mixture in the large bowl in multiple additions, alternating back and forth between the two, starting and ending with the flour mixture and beating on medium speed. Scrape down the sides and bottom of the bowl with a spatula and stir in any unmixed bits of batter.

4. Pour the batter into the prepared Bundt pan. Bake until a toothpick inserted into the center comes out clean, 60 to 75 minutes.

5. Let cool for about 10 minutes and then turn out onto a wire rack to cool completely. Cut and serve.

STORAGE: Will keep tightly covered with plastic wrap or in an airtight container at room temperature for 4 to 5 days.

TOP IT OFF: For a little flair, this cake is wonderful served up with fresh berries and homemade Whipped Cream (page 130).

CREAM CHEESE BUNDT CAKE

This cake is dense and rich, thanks to the cream cheese and butter.
It tastes great served with coffee, either for breakfast or dessert.

PREP TIME: 15 MINUTES • BAKE TIME: 1 HOUR 10 MINUTES • YIELD: 12 SERVINGS

1 cup (2 sticks)
unsalted butter, at
room temperature

1 (8-ounce) package
full-fat cream cheese, at
room temperature

2½ cups
granulated sugar

½ cup full-fat sour cream

1 tablespoon
vanilla extract

6 large eggs

2¼ cups
all-purpose flour

½ teaspoon
baking powder

½ teaspoon baking soda

½ teaspoon salt

1. Preheat the oven to 325°F. Coat a 10-inch (12-cup) Bundt pan with nonstick baking spray with flour.

2. In a large bowl, using an electric mixer on medium speed, beat the butter and cream cheese together until creamy. Add the sugar and beat until light and fluffy. Beat in the sour cream just until combined. Beat in the vanilla, then add the eggs one at a time, beating just until each egg is mixed in.

3. In a medium bowl, sift together the flour, baking powder, baking soda, and salt. Add the dry ingredients to the batter and beat on medium speed just until incorporated into the batter. Scrape down the sides and bottom of the bowl with a spatula and stir in any unmixed bits of batter.

4. Pour the batter into the prepared Bundt pan. Bake until a toothpick inserted into the center comes out clean, about 70 minutes.

5. Let cool for about 10 minutes, then turn out onto a wire rack to cool completely. Cut and serve.

STORAGE: Will keep tightly covered with plastic wrap or in an airtight container in the refrigerator for 3 to 4 days.

TOP IT OFF: For an extra pop of flavor, serve with home-made Whipped Cream (page 130) and fresh berries.

CHEESECAKE-FILLED VANILLA BUNDT CAKE

This vanilla Bundt cake has a soft, tender cheesecake top and a dense, chewy cake base. It's the perfect way to really amp up a Bundt cake.

PREP TIME: 20 MINUTES • BAKE TIME: 1 HOUR 15 MINUTES • YIELD: 12 SERVINGS

FOR THE CHEESECAKE TOP

2 (8-ounce) packages full-fat cream cheese, at room temperature

1 cup granulated sugar

1 teaspoon vanilla extract

1 large egg

FOR THE CAKE

2 cups granulated sugar

1 cup (2 sticks) unsalted butter, at room temperature

1 tablespoon vanilla extract

4 large eggs

2¾ cups all-purpose flour

½ teaspoon baking powder

½ teaspoon baking soda

½ teaspoon salt

1 cup whole milk

1. Preheat the oven to 325°F. Coat a 10-inch (12-cup) Bundt pan with nonstick baking spray with flour.

2. For the cheesecake top, in a medium bowl, using an electric mixer on medium speed, beat the cream cheese and sugar together until smooth. Add the vanilla and egg and beat until the egg is incorporated. Scrape down the sides and stir in any bits of unmixed egg with a spatula. Set aside.

3. For the cake, in a large bowl, using the mixer on medium speed, cream the sugar and butter together until light and fluffy. Beat in the vanilla, then add the eggs, one at a time, beating just until each egg is mixed in. Scrape down the sides and bottom of the bowl and stir in any unmixed bits with a spatula.

4. In another medium bowl, sift together the flour, baking powder, baking soda, and salt. Add the dry ingredients and milk to the butter-sugar mixture in the large bowl in multiple additions, alternating back and forth between the two, starting and ending with the flour mixture and beating on medium speed. Scrape down the sides and bottom of the bowl and stir in any unmixed bits of batter with a spatula.

5. Pour three-quarters of the batter into the prepared Bundt pan. Using a spatula, push the batter up the sides of the pan to form a well in the center of the batter. Spoon the cheesecake mixture into the well. Spoon the rest of the Bundt cake batter on top of the cheesecake. Try to cover the cheesecake batter completely. Bake until a toothpick inserted into the center comes out clean, 60 to 75 minutes.

6. Let cool for about 10 minutes, then turn out onto a wire rack to cool completely. Cut and serve.

STORAGE: Will keep tightly covered in plastic wrap in the refrigerator for up to 3 to 4 days.

TOP IT OFF: This cheesecake has a built-in topping, but if you're looking for more flavor and color, fresh berries of any kind make a great addition.

PIÑA COLADA BUNDT CAKE

This piña colada cake is packed full of flavor from the crushed pineapple and the coconut milk.

PREP TIME: 15 MINUTES • BAKE TIME: 1 HOUR • YIELD: 12 SERVINGS

2 cups granulated sugar

1 cup (2 sticks) unsalted butter, at room temperature

1 tablespoon vanilla extract

1 teaspoon rum extract or 2 tablespoons rum

½ teaspoon coconut extract

4 large eggs

2¾ cups all-purpose flour

½ teaspoon baking powder

½ teaspoon baking soda

½ teaspoon salt

1 cup coconut milk

1 cup crushed pineapple, well drained

1. Preheat the oven to 325°F. Coat a 10-inch (12-cup) Bundt pan with nonstick baking spray with flour.

2. In a large bowl, using an electric mixer on medium speed, cream the sugar and butter together until light and fluffy. Beat in the vanilla and rum and coconut extracts, then add the eggs, one at a time, beating just until each egg is mixed in.

3. In a medium bowl, sift together the flour, baking powder, baking soda, and salt. Add the dry ingredients and coconut milk to the butter-sugar mixture in the large bowl in multiple additions, alternating back and forth between the two, starting and ending with the flour mixture and beating on medium speed. Scrape down the sides and bottom of the bowl and stir in any unmixed bits of batter with a spatula. Fold in the crushed pineapple until evenly distributed.

4. Pour the batter into the prepared Bundt pan. Bake until a toothpick inserted into the center comes out clean, about 1 hour.

5. Let cool for about 10 minutes, then turn out onto a wire rack to cool completely. Cut and serve.

STORAGE: Will keep tightly covered with plastic wrap or in an airtight container at room temperature for 4 to 5 days.

TIP: Drain the crushed pineapple by putting it in a fine-mesh strainer and pressing down with a spatula.

CHERRY 7UP BUNDT CAKE

This brightly flavored Bundt cake is for maraschino cherry lovers.

PREP TIME: 15 MINUTES • BAKE TIME: 1 HOUR • YIELD: 12 SERVINGS

2 cups granulated sugar

1 cup (2 sticks) unsalted butter, at room temperature

1 tablespoon grated lemon zest

1 tablespoon grated lime zest

1 tablespoon vanilla extract

1 teaspoon cherry extract

5 large eggs

2½ cups all-purpose flour

½ teaspoon baking powder

½ teaspoon baking soda

½ teaspoon salt

¾ cup 7UP

¾ cup maraschino cherries, drained and chopped

1. Preheat the oven to 325°F. Coat a 10-inch (12-cup) Bundt pan with nonstick baking spray with flour.

2. In a large bowl, using an electric mixer on medium speed, cream the sugar and butter together until light and fluffy. Beat in the lemon and lime zests, vanilla, and cherry extract, then add the eggs, one at a time, beating just until each egg is mixed in. Scrape down the sides and bottom of the bowl and stir in any unmixed bits with a spatula.

3. In a medium bowl, sift together the flour, baking powder, baking soda, and salt. Add the dry ingredients and 7UP to the butter-sugar mixture in the large bowl in multiple additions, alternating back and forth between the two, starting and ending with the flour mixture and beating on medium speed. Scrape down the sides and bottom of the bowl and stir in any unmixed bits of batter with a spatula. Fold in the chopped cherries.

4. Pour the batter into the prepared Bundt pan. Bake until a toothpick inserted into the center comes out clean, about 1 hour. Let cool for about 10 minutes, then turn out onto a wire rack to cool completely. Cut and serve.

STORAGE: Will keep in an airtight container or tightly covered in plastic wrap at room temperature for 4 to 5 days.

TOP IT OFF: Drizzle 2 to 3 tablespoons of the maraschino cherry juice on top of the cake for color and yet another hit of cherry flavor.

CARROT CAKE BUNDT CAKE

This cake is tender, moist, and full of spicy flavor.
While it's baking, the aroma will remind you of a crisp fall day.
It's a great dessert to serve for the holidays, too.

PREP TIME: 20 MINUTES ● BAKE TIME: 1 HOUR ● YIELD: 12 SERVINGS

1 cup granulated sugar

1 cup packed light
brown sugar

2 teaspoons
ground cinnamon

½ teaspoon
ground nutmeg

¼ teaspoon
ground cloves

1¼ cups vegetable oil

2 teaspoons
vanilla extract

4 large eggs

2½ cups
all-purpose flour

1 teaspoon
baking powder

2 teaspoons baking soda

½ teaspoon salt

3 cups grated
carrots (about
4 medium carrots)

1. Preheat the oven to 325°F. Coat a 10-inch (12-cup) Bundt pan with nonstick baking spray with flour.

2. In a large bowl, combine the granulated and brown sugars, cinnamon, nutmeg, and cloves. Add the oil, vanilla, and eggs and whisk together until fully incorporated.

3. In a medium bowl, sift together the flour, baking powder, baking soda, and salt. Pour the dry ingredients into the wet mixture. Mix on low speed with an electric mixer until the flour is almost completely incorporated. Increase the speed to medium and mix for 30 seconds. Fold in the carrots until evenly distributed.

4. Pour the batter into the prepared Bundt pan. Bake until a toothpick inserted into the center comes out clean, about 1 hour.

5. Let cool for about 10 minutes, then turn out onto a wire rack to cool completely. Cut and serve.

STORAGE: Will keep tightly covered in plastic wrap or in an airtight container at room temperature for 4 to 5 days.

TOP IT OFF: Dust the top with powdered sugar or drizzle it with warm store-bought caramel sauce.

CHOCOLATE
PEANUT BUTTER BUNDT CAKE

This super-dense cake is incredibly moist, full of flavor, and highly addictive! It comes together quickly and doesn't require anything fancier than a whisk.

PREP TIME: 15 MINUTES • BAKE TIME: 1 HOUR 15 MINUTES • YIELD: 12 SERVINGS

1 cup strongly
brewed coffee

¾ cup (1½ sticks)
unsalted butter, cubed

2 tablespoons
vegetable oil

¾ cup unsweetened
cocoa powder

1 cup full-fat sour cream

2 teaspoons
vanilla extract

1 cup creamy
peanut butter

2 large eggs,
lightly beaten

2 cups all-purpose flour

2 cups granulated sugar

½ teaspoon
baking powder

1½ teaspoons
baking soda

½ teaspoon salt

1. Preheat the oven to 325°F. Coat a 10-inch (12-cup) Bundt pan with nonstick baking spray with flour.

2. In a medium microwave-safe bowl, microwave the coffee and butter for 2 to 2½ minutes on high, until the butter is completely melted. Whisk in the oil, add the cocoa and whisk until creamy. Whisk in the sour cream and vanilla until combined. Whisk in the peanut butter until incorporated. Whisk in the eggs until incorporated. Set aside.

3. In a large bowl, combine the flour, sugar, baking powder, baking soda, and salt. Add the chocolate mixture and stir until well combined.

4. Pour the batter into the prepared Bundt pan. Bake until a toothpick inserted into the center comes out clean, about 75 minutes.

5. Let cool for about 10 minutes, then turn out onto a wire rack to cool completely. Cut and serve.

STORAGE: Will keep tightly covered in plastic wrap or in an airtight container at room temperature for 4 to 5 days.

TOP IT OFF: While this cake is perfect on its own, it is spectacular glazed with Chocolate Peanut Butter Ganache (page 126).

MINT CHOCOLATE CHIP BUNDT CAKE

If you like, you can omit the food coloring, but I love the shade of green it turns this flavorful cake.

PREP TIME: 15 MINUTES • BAKE TIME: 1 HOUR • YIELD: 12 SERVINGS

2 cups granulated sugar

1 cup (2 sticks) unsalted butter, at room temperature

1 tablespoon vanilla extract

1½ teaspoons mint extract

4 large eggs

2¾ cups all-purpose flour

½ teaspoon baking powder

½ teaspoon baking soda

½ teaspoon salt

1 cup whole milk

½ teaspoon green gel food coloring (optional)

1¼ cups mini chocolate chips, divided

1. Preheat the oven to 325°F. Coat a 10-inch (12-cup) Bundt pan with nonstick baking spray with flour.

2. In a large bowl, using an electric mixer on medium speed, cream the sugar and butter together until light and fluffy. Beat in the vanilla and mint extract, then add the eggs, one at a time, beating just until each egg is incorporated. Scrape down the sides and bottom of the bowl and stir in any unmixed eggs with a spatula.

3. In a medium bowl, sift together the flour, baking powder, baking soda, and salt. Add the dry ingredients, milk, and food coloring, if using, to the butter-sugar mixture in the large bowl in multiple additions, alternating back and forth between the two, starting and ending with the flour mixture and beating on medium speed. Scrape down the sides and bottom of the bowl and stir in any unmixed bits of batter with a spatula.

4. Pour three-quarters of the batter into the prepared Bundt pan. Sprinkle 1 cup of the chocolate chips on top of the batter. Pour the remaining batter on top of the chips. Sprinkle the remaining ¼ cup of chips on top of the batter. Bake until a toothpick inserted into the center comes out clean, about 1 hour.

5. Let cool for about 10 minutes, then turn out onto a wire rack to cool completely. Cut and serve.

STORAGE: Will keep tightly covered with plastic wrap or in an airtight container at room temperature for 4 to 5 days.

TOP IT OFF: If you want even more chocolatey, minty flavor, top this with Mint Chocolate Ganache (page 126).

CINNAMON SWIRL BUNDT CAKE

This Bundt cake consists of a dense cream cheese cake with a thick swirl of cinnamon sugar in the center. It tastes similar to a cinnamon roll and is best when served with a hot cup of coffee.

PREP TIME: 15 MINUTES • BAKE TIME: 1 HOUR 10 MINUTES • YIELD: 12 SERVINGS

**FOR THE
CINNAMON SUGAR**

¼ cup granulated sugar

¼ cup packed light
brown sugar

1½ tablespoons
ground cinnamon

FOR THE CAKE

1 cup (2 sticks)
unsalted butter, at
room temperature

1 (8-ounce) package
full-fat cream cheese, at
room temperature

2½ cups
granulated sugar

½ cup full-fat sour cream

1 tablespoon
vanilla extract

6 large eggs

1. Preheat the oven to 325°F. Coat a 10-inch (12-cup) Bundt pan with nonstick baking spray with flour.

2. For the cinnamon sugar, in a small bowl, combine the granulated and brown sugars and cinnamon. Set aside.

3. For the cake, in a large bowl, using an electric mixer on medium speed, beat the butter and cream cheese together until smooth. Add the sugar and beat until light and fluffy. Beat in the sour cream just until combined. Beat in the vanilla, then add the eggs, one at a time, beating just until each egg is incorporated. Scrape down the sides and bottom of the bowl and stir in any unmixed eggs with a spatula.

4. In a medium bowl, sift together the flour, baking powder, baking soda, and salt. Add the dry ingredients to the butter-sugar mixture in the large bowl and beat with the mixer on medium speed just until incorporated into the batter. Scrape down the sides and bottom of the bowl and stir in any unmixed bits of batter with the spatula.

5. Pour three-quarters of the batter into the prepared Bundt pan. Sprinkle the cinnamon sugar evenly on top of the batter. Spoon the remaining batter on top of the cinnamon sugar. (Note: If you would like a swirl, drag a knife through the batter and

**2 ¼ cups
all-purpose flour**

**½ teaspoon
baking powder**

½ teaspoon baking soda

½ teaspoon salt

cinnamon-sugar layer a couple of times.) Bake until a toothpick inserted into the center comes out clean, about 70 minutes.

6. Let cool for about 10 minutes, then turn out onto a wire rack to cool completely. Cut and serve.

STORAGE: Will keep tightly covered with plastic wrap or in an airtight container at room temperature for 4 to 5 days.

TOP IT OFF: For a little extra something, dust the top of the Bundt cake with powdered sugar before serving.

APPLE BUTTER BUNDT CAKE

Apple butter is a go-to for my family every fall. This cake is incredibly moist and spiced from the apple butter and dense from the cream cheese.

PREP TIME: 15 MINUTES • BAKE TIME: 1 HOUR 15 MINUTES • YIELD: 12 SERVINGS

1 cup (2 sticks) unsalted butter, at room temperature

1 (8-ounce) package full-fat cream cheese, at room temperature

1½ cups granulated sugar

1 cup packed light brown sugar

1½ cups apple butter

1 tablespoon vanilla extract

6 large eggs

2¼ cups all-purpose flour

½ teaspoon baking powder

½ teaspoon baking soda

½ teaspoon salt

1 teaspoon ground cinnamon

¼ teaspoon ground allspice

1. Preheat the oven to 325°F. Coat a 10-inch (12-cup) Bundt pan with nonstick baking spray with flour.

2. In a large bowl, using an electric mixer on medium speed, beat the butter and cream cheese together until smooth. Add the granulated and brown sugars and beat until light and fluffy. Beat in the apple butter and vanilla, then add the eggs, one at a time, beating just until each egg is incorporated. Scrape down the sides and bottom of the bowl and stir in any unmixed eggs with a spatula.

3. In a medium bowl, sift together the flour, baking powder, baking soda, salt, cinnamon, and allspice. Add the dry ingredients to the batter and beat with the mixer on medium speed just until incorporated into the batter. Scrape down the sides and bottom of the bowl to get any unmixed bits of batter.

4. Pour the batter into the prepared Bundt pan. Bake until a toothpick inserted in the center comes out clean, about 75 minutes.

5. Let cool for about 10 minutes, then turn out onto a wire rack to cool completely. Cut and serve.

STORAGE: Will keep tightly covered with plastic wrap or in an airtight container at room temperature for 4 to 5 days.

TOP IT OFF: Dust the top with powdered sugar.

FRESH STRAWBERRY BUNDT CAKE

This cake is a deep pink color from the strawberry purée, with little bits of strawberry throughout. For an extra punch of flavor, strawberry extract is added.

PREP TIME: 15 MINUTES • BAKE TIME: 1 HOUR • YIELD: 12 SERVINGS

2 cups granulated sugar

1 cup (2 sticks) unsalted butter, at room temperature

1 tablespoon vanilla extract

2 teaspoons strawberry extract

4 large eggs

2¾ cups all-purpose flour

½ teaspoon baking powder

½ teaspoon baking soda

½ teaspoon salt

½ cup whole milk

½ teaspoon red gel food coloring (optional)

1 cup strawberry purée (about 2 cups strawberries, hulled, puréed, and strained)

1. Preheat the oven to 325°F. Coat a 10-inch (12-cup) Bundt pan with nonstick baking spray with flour.

2. In a large bowl, using an electric mixer on medium speed, cream the sugar and butter together until light and fluffy. Beat in the vanilla and strawberry extract, then add the eggs, one at a time, beating just until each egg is incorporated. Scrape down the sides and bottom of the bowl with a spatula and stir in any unmixed bits.

3. In a medium bowl, sift together the flour, baking powder, baking soda, and salt.

4. Whisk the milk and food coloring (if using) into the strawberry purée.

5. Alternately add the dry ingredients and strawberry purée to the butter-sugar mixture in the large bowl in multiple additions, beginning and ending with the flour mixture and beating on medium speed. Scrape down the sides and bottom of the bowl to get any unmixed bits of batter.

CONTINUED ▶

FRESH STRAWBERRY BUNDT CAKE

continued

6. Pour the batter into the prepared Bundt pan. Bake until a toothpick inserted into the center comes out clean, about 1 hour.

7. Let cool for about 10 minutes, then turn out onto a wire rack to cool completely. Cut and serve.

STORAGE: Will keep tightly covered with plastic wrap or in an airtight container at room temperature for 4 to 5 days.

TOP IT OFF: This is the perfect summer dessert when served with a dollop of homemade Whipped Cream (page 130) and a few slices of fresh strawberries.

MEXICAN CHOCOLATE BUNDT CAKE

This cake has a rich chocolate flavor with a hint of cinnamon and it finishes with a punch of heat. Serve it up with a tall glass of milk.

PREP TIME: 15 MINUTES • BAKE TIME: 1 HOUR • YIELD: 12 SERVINGS

1 cup strongly brewed coffee

¾ cup (1½ sticks) unsalted butter, cubed

2 tablespoons vegetable oil

¾ cup unsweetened cocoa powder

1 cup full-fat sour cream

2 teaspoons vanilla extract

2 cups all-purpose flour

1½ cups granulated sugar

½ teaspoon baking powder

1½ teaspoons baking soda

1½ teaspoons ground cinnamon

½ teaspoon salt

¼ teaspoon cayenne pepper

2 large eggs, lightly beaten

1. Preheat the oven to 325°F. Coat a 10-inch (12-cup) Bundt pan with nonstick baking spray with flour.

2. In a medium microwave-safe bowl, microwave the coffee and butter for 2 to 2½ minutes on high, until the butter is completely melted. Whisk in the oil, then whisk in the cocoa until creamy. Whisk in the sour cream and vanilla until combined. Set aside.

3. In a large bowl, combine the flour, sugar, baking powder, baking soda, cinnamon, salt, and cayenne. Add the cocoa mixture and eggs and whisk until fully incorporated and smooth.

4. Pour the batter into the prepared Bundt pan. Bake until a toothpick inserted into the center comes out clean, 53 to 60 minutes.

5. Let cool for about 10 minutes, then turn out onto a wire rack to cool completely. Cut and serve.

STORAGE: Will keep tightly covered with plastic wrap or in an airtight container at room temperature for 4 to 5 days.

TIP: For a little more heat, add another ¼ to ½ teaspoon of cayenne pepper.

TOP IT OFF: For even more chocolate flavor, glaze with Mexican Chocolate Ganache (page 126).

COFFEE BUNDT CAKE

Are you ready for an intense coffee-flavored cake? This will become a go-to for all coffee lovers. It's sweet, dense, moist, and highly addictive.

PREP TIME: 15 MINUTES • BAKE TIME: 1 HOUR • YIELD: 12 SERVINGS

2¼ cups
granulated sugar

1 cup (2 sticks)
unsalted butter, at
room temperature

3 tablespoons instant
coffee granules

1 tablespoon hot water

¼ cup full-fat sour cream

1 tablespoon
vanilla extract

3 large eggs

2¾ cups
all-purpose flour

½ teaspoon
baking powder

½ teaspoon baking soda

½ teaspoon salt

1 cup buttermilk

1. Preheat the oven to 325°F. Coat a 10-inch (12-cup) Bundt pan with nonstick baking spray with flour.

2. In a large bowl, using an electric mixer on medium speed, cream the sugar and butter together until light and fluffy.

3. In a small bowl, stir together the instant coffee and hot water until the granules dissolve. Beat the coffee mixture into the butter-sugar mixture until incorporated. Beat in the sour cream and vanilla, then add the eggs, one at a time, beating until each egg is incorporated. Scrape down the sides and bottom of the bowl with a spatula and stir in any unmixed bits.

4. In a medium bowl, sift together the flour, baking powder, baking soda, and salt. Add the dry ingredients and buttermilk to the butter-sugar mixture in the large bowl in multiple additions, alternating back and forth between the two, starting and ending with the flour mixture and beating on medium speed. Scrape down the sides and bottom of the bowl with a spatula and stir in any unmixed bits of batter.

5. Pour the batter into the prepared Bundt pan. Bake until a toothpick inserted into the center comes out clean, about 1 hour.

6. Let cool for about 10 minutes, then turn out onto a wire rack to cool completely. Slice and serve.

STORAGE: Will keep tightly wrapped in plastic wrap or in an airtight container at room temperature for 4 to 5 days.

TOP IT OFF: If you think some coffee flavor is good but more coffee flavor is better, coat the cake with Coffee Glaze (page 128).

GINGERBREAD BUNDT CAKE

Need a new go-to Christmas cake? This gingerbread Bundt cake is your recipe.

PREP TIME: 15 MINUTES • BAKE TIME: 1 HOUR 5 MINUTES • YIELD: 12 SERVINGS

1 cup (2 sticks) unsalted butter, at room temperature

1¼ cups packed light brown sugar

1 cup granulated sugar

¾ cup dark (not blackstrap) molasses

2 teaspoons vanilla extract

3 large eggs

2¾ cups all-purpose flour

1 tablespoon ground ginger

2 teaspoons ground cinnamon

½ teaspoon baking powder

½ teaspoon baking soda

½ teaspoon salt

1 cup buttermilk

1. Preheat the oven to 325°F. Coat a 10-inch (12-cup) Bundt pan with nonstick baking spray with flour.

2. In a large bowl, using an electric mixer on medium speed, cream the butter and brown and granulated sugars together until light and fluffy. Beat in the molasses and vanilla, then add the eggs, one at a time, beating just until each egg is incorporated. Scrape down the sides and bottom of the bowl with a spatula and stir in any unmixed bits.

3. In a medium bowl, sift together the flour, ginger, cinnamon, baking powder, baking soda, and salt. Add the dry ingredients and buttermilk to the butter-sugar mixture in the large bowl in multiple additions, alternating back and forth between the two, starting and ending with the flour mixture and beating on medium speed. Scrape down the sides and bottom of the bowl with a spatula and stir in any unmixed bits of batter.

4. Pour the batter into the prepared Bundt pan. Bake until a toothpick inserted into the center comes out clean, about 65 minutes.

5. Let cool for about 10 minutes, then turn out onto a wire rack to cool completely. Cut and serve.

STORAGE: Will keep tightly covered in plastic wrap or in an airtight container at room temperature for 4 to 5 days.

TOP IT OFF: Dust it with powdered sugar before slicing.

LEMON PUDDING BUNDT CAKE

The lemon in this cake is a triple threat: It boasts lemon juice and zest and instant lemon pudding.

PREP TIME: 15 MINUTES • BAKE TIME: 1 HOUR 5 MINUTES • YIELD: 12 SERVINGS

2 cups granulated sugar

1 cup (2 sticks) unsalted butter, at room temperature

1 tablespoon grated lemon zest

1 teaspoon vanilla extract

3 large eggs

2¾ cups all-purpose flour

1 (3.4-ounce) box dry instant lemon pudding mix

½ teaspoon baking powder

½ teaspoon baking soda

¼ cup fresh lemon juice

1 cup buttermilk

1. Preheat the oven to 325°F. Coat a 10-inch (12-cup) Bundt pan with nonstick baking spray with flour.

2. In a large bowl, using an electric mixer on medium speed, cream the sugar and butter together until light and fluffy. Beat in the lemon zest and vanilla, then add the eggs, one at a time, beating just until each egg is incorporated. Scrape down the bowl with a spatula and stir in any unmixed bits.

3. In a medium bowl, sift together the flour, lemon pudding mix, baking powder, and baking soda.

4. Whisk the lemon juice into the buttermilk. Add the dry ingredients and buttermilk to the butter-sugar mixture in the large bowl in multiple additions, alternating back and forth, starting and ending with the flour mixture and beating on medium speed. Scrape down the sides and bottom of the bowl with a spatula and stir in any unmixed bits of batter.

5. Pour the batter into the prepared Bundt pan. Bake until a toothpick inserted into the center comes out clean, about 65 minutes. Let cool for about 10 minutes, then turn out onto a wire rack to cool completely. Cut and serve.

STORAGE: Will keep tightly covered in plastic wrap or in an airtight container at room temperature for 4 to 5 days.

TOP IT OFF: Lemon Glaze (page 128) will give this cake extra tangy flavor, if desired.

CHOCOLATE-BANANA SWIRL BUNDT CAKE

This incredibly moist cake is the perfect way to use up overripe bananas. It has swirls of chocolate and big banana flavor. It tastes amazing warmed up and slathered with butter.

PREP TIME: 20 MINUTES • BAKE TIME: 1 HOUR • YIELD: 12 SERVINGS

1 cup (2 sticks) unsalted butter, at room temperature

1 cup granulated sugar

1 cup packed light brown sugar

1¾ cups mashed overripe bananas (about 4 bananas)

1 cup full-fat sour cream

1 tablespoon vanilla extract

3 large eggs

3 cups all-purpose flour

½ teaspoon baking powder

1½ teaspoons baking soda

½ teaspoon salt

2 tablespoons unsweetened cocoa powder

1. Preheat the oven to 325°F. Coat a 10-inch (12-cup) Bundt pan with nonstick baking spray with flour.

2. In a large bowl, using an electric mixer on medium speed, cream the butter and granulated and brown sugars together until light and fluffy. Beat in the bananas and sour cream just until the sour cream is worked into the batter. Beat in the vanilla, then add the eggs, one at a time, beating just until each egg is incorporated. Scrape down the sides and bottom of the bowl and stir in any unmixed eggs with a spatula.

3. In a medium bowl, sift together the flour, baking powder, baking soda, and salt. Add the dry ingredients to the batter and beat with the mixer on medium speed just until incorporated into the batter. Scrape down the sides and bottom of the bowl to get any unmixed bits of batter.

4. Transfer 2 cups of the batter to a small bowl, add the cocoa, and beat on medium speed, just until it is incorporated into the batter. Pour the chocolate-banana batter back into the bowl with the banana batter. Fold the batter together four to six times so the chocolate is swirled throughout the batter but not fully mixed in.

5. Pour the batter into the prepared Bundt pan. Bake until a toothpick inserted into the center comes out clean, about 1 hour.

6. Let cool for about 10 minutes, then turn out onto a wire rack to cool completely. Cut and serve.

STORAGE: Will keep tightly covered in plastic wrap or in an airtight container at room temperature for 4 to 5 days.

VARIATION: Walnuts are a great addition to this cake. Add ¾ cup chopped walnuts to the chocolate-banana batter.

TOP IT OFF: This is delicious drizzled with warm store-bought caramel sauce.

Raspberry White Chocolate
Loaf Cake, page 81

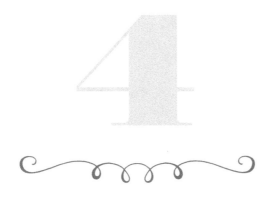

SNACKING CAKES

Cake bars and loaf cakes are the best kind of snacking cakes. No frostings or glazes are required, but they are always a welcome addition. All of these recipes make a nice grab-and-go cake for when you're on the run. Grab a piece of cake and walk away without needing a plate or fork.

There is a nice variety of cakes included in this chapter. You're bound to find a cake that's perfect for the occasion.

APPLESAUCE SNACK CAKE

This tender snack cake is perfect for fall. It's loaded with warm spices: cinnamon, nutmeg, and cloves. Add the optional walnuts and raisins for the ultimate applesauce snack cake.

PREP TIME: 15 MINUTES • BAKE TIME: 45 MINUTES • YIELD: 9 SERVINGS

½ cup (1 stick) unsalted butter, at room temperature

¾ cup granulated sugar

¼ cup packed light brown sugar

1 cup sweetened applesauce

2 cups all-purpose flour

1 teaspoon baking soda

1 teaspoon ground cinnamon

¼ teaspoon ground cloves

⅛ teaspoon ground nutmeg

¼ teaspoon salt

½ cup chopped walnuts (optional)

½ cup raisins (optional)

1. Preheat the oven to 350°F. Coat an 8-inch square baking pan with nonstick baking spray with flour.

2. In a large bowl, using an electric mixer on medium speed, cream the butter and granulated and brown sugars together until light and fluffy. Beat in the applesauce until combined.

3. In a medium bowl, combine the flour, baking soda, cinnamon, cloves, nutmeg, and salt until the spices are evenly distributed.

4. Add the dry ingredients to the butter-sugar mixture in the large bowl, using the mixer on medium speed, and beat in just until combined. Fold in the walnuts and raisins (if using).

5. Pour the batter into the prepared baking pan. Bake until a toothpick inserted into the center comes out clean, 40 to 45 minutes.

6. Let the cake cool completely. Cut into three strips lengthwise and three strips widthwise for 9 servings.

STORAGE: Will keep tightly covered with plastic wrap or in an airtight container at room temperature for 4 to 5 days.

TOP IT OFF: To add an extra layer of sweetness, dust the top with powdered sugar before serving.

ZUCCHINI CHOCOLATE CHIP LOAF CAKE

This zucchini loaf cake is moist and flavorful. There's a nice bit of chocolate worked into each slice of cake. It tastes great served warm with butter.

PREP TIME: 15 MINUTES • BAKE TIME: 1 HOUR 20 MINUTES • YIELD: 12 SERVINGS

½ cup vegetable oil

¾ cup granulated sugar

⅓ cup packed light brown sugar

2 teaspoons vanilla extract

3 large eggs

2 cups shredded zucchini (about 2 medium zucchini)

2 cups all-purpose flour

½ teaspoon baking powder

½ teaspoon baking soda

¼ teaspoon salt

¼ cup milk chocolate chips

1. Preheat the oven to 350°F. Line an 8½-by-4½-inch loaf pan with heavy-duty aluminum foil or parchment paper. Coat the foil or parchment with a nonstick baking spray.

2. In a large bowl, using an electric mixer on medium speed, beat the oil, granulated and brown sugars, vanilla, and eggs together until well combined. Add the zucchini and beat until fully incorporated.

3. In another large bowl, combine the flour, baking powder, baking soda, and salt. Add the zucchini mixture and whisk until the batter is smooth. Fold in the chocolate chips.

4. Pour the batter into the prepared loaf pan. Bake until a toothpick inserted into the center comes out clean, about 80 minutes.

5. Let the cake cool completely, then turn out onto a serving plate. Cut and serve.

STORAGE: Will keep tightly covered with plastic wrap or in an airtight container at room temperature for 4 to 5 days.

TOP IT OFF: Drizzle with Chocolate Ganache (page 126) before slicing.

APPLE FRITTER LOAF CAKE

Have you ever had an apple fritter? This loaf cake tastes just like one but is so much easier to whip up. The cake's chunks of apple and swirls of cinnamon and sugar make for a delectable snack anytime.

PREP TIME: 15 MINUTES • BAKE TIME: 1 HOUR 5 MINUTES • YIELD: 12 SERVINGS

FOR THE CINNAMON SUGAR

⅓ cup packed light brown sugar

2 teaspoons ground cinnamon

FOR THE CAKE

¾ cup granulated sugar

½ cup (1 stick) unsalted butter, at room temperature

2 teaspoons vanilla extract

2 large eggs

1½ cups all-purpose flour

1 teaspoon baking powder

1 teaspoon baking soda

¼ teaspoon salt

½ cup buttermilk

1. Preheat the oven to 350°F. Line an 8½-by-4½-inch loaf pan with heavy-duty aluminum foil or parchment paper. Coat the foil or parchment with nonstick baking spray. Set aside.

2. For the cinnamon sugar, in a small bowl, combine the brown sugar and cinnamon. Set aside.

3. For the cake, in a large bowl, using an electric mixer on medium speed, cream the sugar and butter together until light and fluffy. Beat in the vanilla, then add the eggs, one at a time, beating just until each egg is incorporated. Scrape down the sides and bottom of the bowl.

4. In a medium bowl, combine the flour, baking powder, baking soda, and salt. Add the dry ingredients and buttermilk to the butter-sugar mixture in the large bowl, alternating back and forth between the two, starting and ending with flour and beating on medium speed. Scrape down the sides and bottom of the bowl with a spatula and stir in any unmixed bits of batter.

5. For the apples, in another medium bowl, combine the sugar and cinnamon. Add the apples and toss until the apples are coated with the cinnamon sugar.

FOR THE APPLES

3 tablespoons
granulated sugar

1½ teaspoons
ground cinnamon

1¾ cups chopped peeled
baking apples

6. Add half of the batter to the prepared loaf pan. Add half of the apples in a layer and gently push them down into the batter. Sprinkle half of the cinnamon sugar over the apples. Repeat, adding the remaining batter, apples, and cinnamon sugar. Use a skewer to swirl it all together. Bake until a toothpick inserted into the center comes out clean, 60 to 65 minutes.

7. Let the cake cool completely, then turn out onto a serving plate. Cut and serve.

STORAGE: Will keep tightly covered with plastic wrap or in an airtight container at room temperature for 4 to 5 days.

TOP IT OFF: This is especially delicious when drizzled with Cream Cheese Glaze (page 127).

BANANA CREAM CHEESE LOAF CAKE

This takes banana bread to another level with cream cheese swirled in, giving it a creamy, cheesecake flavor.

PREP TIME: 20 MINUTES • BAKE TIME: 1 HOUR 20 MINUTES • YIELD: 12 SERVINGS

FOR THE CREAM CHEESE LAYER

1 (8-ounce package) full-fat cream cheese, at room temperature

½ cup granulated sugar

1 teaspoon vanilla extract

1 large egg

1 tablespoon all-purpose flour

FOR THE CAKE

¾ cup ripe mashed bananas (about 2 bananas)

¾ cup packed light brown sugar

⅓ cup unsalted butter, melted

⅓ cup full-fat sour cream

2 teaspoons vanilla extract

1. Preheat the oven to 350°F. Line an 8½-by-4½-inch loaf pan with heavy-duty aluminum foil or parchment paper. Coat the foil or parchment with nonstick baking spray. Set aside.

2. For the cream cheese layer, in a medium bowl, using an electric mixer on medium speed, beat the cream cheese and sugar together until creamy. Add the vanilla and egg, and beat until combined. Add the flour and beat just until it's worked into the batter. Set aside.

3. For the cake, in a large bowl, using the mixer on medium speed, beat the banana, brown sugar, and melted butter together until combined. Beat in the sour cream, vanilla, and eggs until fully incorporated.

4. In a medium bowl, combine the flour, baking powder, baking soda, and salt. Add to the banana mixture and beat on medium speed, just until the flour is incorporated.

5. Pour half of the batter into the prepared loaf pan. Dollop the cream cheese mixture over the top of the banana batter. Gently spread it out to cover any spots of batter still showing through. Pour the remaining banana batter on top of the cream cheese layer. Spread it out to cover the cream cheese layer. Use a butter knife or skewer and gently swirl the

2 large eggs

1½ cups all-purpose flour

¼ teaspoon
baking powder

½ teaspoon baking soda

¼ teaspoon salt

cream cheese layer and banana batter together. Bake until a toothpick inserted into the center comes out clean, 75 to 80 minutes.

6. Let the cake cool completely, then turn it out onto a serving plate. Cut and serve.

STORAGE: Will keep tightly covered with plastic wrap or in an airtight container at room temperature for 3 to 4 days.

TOP IT OFF: Double up on the cream cheese and top this with Cream Cheese Glaze (page 127).

PEANUT BUTTER CHOCOLATE CHIP SNACK CAKE

Peanut butter lovers will love this snack—it tastes like an extra-thick peanut butter cookie with a generous smattering of chocolate chips throughout for an extra-sweet treat.

PREP TIME: 10 MINUTES • BAKE TIME: 45 MINUTES • YIELD: 9 SERVINGS

¾ cup creamy peanut butter

½ cup (1 stick) unsalted butter, melted

½ cup granulated sugar

½ cup packed light brown sugar

1 teaspoon vanilla extract

2 large eggs

1 cup all-purpose flour

¼ teaspoon baking powder

½ teaspoon baking soda

¼ teaspoon salt

¼ cup whole milk

½ cup milk chocolate chips, divided

1. Preheat the oven to 350°F. Coat an 8-inch square baking pan with nonstick baking spray with flour.

2. In a large bowl, using an electric mixer on medium speed, beat the peanut butter, butter, and granulated and brown sugars together until creamy. Beat in the vanilla, then add the eggs, one at a time, beating just until each egg is incorporated.

3. In a medium bowl, combine the flour, baking powder, baking soda, and salt. Add the dry ingredients and milk to the butter-sugar mixture in the large bowl, alternating back and forth between the two, starting and ending with the flour mixture and beating on medium speed. Scrape down the sides and bottom of the bowl with a spatula and stir in any unmixed bits of batter. Fold half the chocolate chips into the batter.

4. Pour the batter into the prepared baking pan and sprinkle the remaining chips on top of the batter. Bake until a toothpick inserted in the center comes out clean, 40 to 45 minutes.

5. Let the cake cool completely before removing it from the pan. Once cooled, cut into three strips lengthwise and three strips widthwise for 9 servings.

STORAGE: Will keep tightly covered with plastic wrap or in an airtight container at room temperature for 4 to 5 days.

TOP IT OFF: You can amp up the peanut butter by drizzling the cake with Peanut Butter Glaze (page 129).

LEMON POPPY SEED LOAF CAKE

This has a pleasant sweet-and-tart flavor that makes it the perfect summer cake to serve up to friends and family.

PREP TIME: 15 MINUTES • BAKE TIME: 1 HOUR 10 MINUTES • YIELD: 12 SERVINGS

1 cup granulated sugar

½ cup vegetable oil

2 large eggs

1 cup full-fat sour cream

¼ cup fresh lemon juice

1 tablespoon grated lemon zest

1 teaspoon vanilla extract

1¾ cups all-purpose flour

¼ cup poppy seeds

2 teaspoons baking powder

¼ teaspoon salt

1. Preheat the oven to 350°F. Line an 8½-by-4½-inch loaf pan with heavy-duty aluminum foil or parchment paper. Coat the foil or parchment with nonstick baking spray. Set aside.

2. In a medium bowl, using an electric mixer on medium speed, beat the sugar and oil together until combined. Add the eggs, sour cream, lemon juice and zest, and vanilla, and beat just until the eggs are incorporated.

3. In a large bowl, combine the flour, poppy seeds, baking powder, and salt. Add the sour cream mixture and beat on medium, just until the flour is worked into the batter.

4. Pour the batter into the prepared loaf pan. Bake until a toothpick inserted into the center comes out clean, 60 to 70 minutes.

5. Let the cake cool completely, then turn out onto a serving plate. Cut and serve.

STORAGE: Will keep tightly covered with plastic wrap or in an airtight container at room temperature for 4 to 5 days.

TOP IT OFF: Lemon Glaze is a nice addition (page 128).

CHERRY CHOCOLATE CHIP LOAF CAKE

This recipe is for the crazy maraschino cherry lovers like myself.

PREP TIME: 15 MINUTES • BAKE TIME: 1 HOUR 20 MINUTES • YIELD: 12 SERVINGS

½ cup vegetable oil

1 cup granulated sugar

1 cup full-fat sour cream

¼ cup maraschino cherry juice (drained from the jar of cherries, below)

1 teaspoon vanilla extract

2 large eggs

1¾ cups all-purpose flour

2 teaspoons baking powder

¼ teaspoon salt

1 (16-ounce) jar maraschino cherries, drained and minced (1 cup minced)

½ cup milk chocolate chips

1. Preheat the oven to 350°F. Line an 8½-by-4½-inch loaf pan with heavy-duty aluminum foil or parchment paper. Coat the foil or parchment with nonstick baking spray. Set aside.

2. In a medium bowl, using an electric mixer on medium speed, beat the oil and sugar together until combined. Beat in the sour cream, cherry juice, vanilla, and eggs just until the eggs are incorporated.

3. In a large bowl, combine the flour, baking powder, and salt. Add the sour cream mixture and beat on medium speed, just until worked into a batter. Fold in the cherries and chips until evenly distributed.

4. Pour the batter into the prepared loaf pan. Bake until a toothpick inserted in the center comes out clean, 75 to 80 minutes.

5. Let the cake cool completely, then turn out onto a serving plate. Cut and serve.

STORAGE: Will keep tightly covered with plastic wrap or in an airtight container at room temperature for 4 to 5 days.

TIP: Dry the maraschino cherries off with a paper towel before mincing them in a mini food processor.

TOP IT OFF: Maraschino Cherry Glaze (page 128) makes a nice addition to this cake.

HOT COCOA SNACK CAKE

Taking a bite of this cake is like taking a drink of hot cocoa. It's chocolatey with marshmallow bits in it. I love using Swiss Miss Marshmallow Lovers hot cocoa mix because it has separate envelopes for the cocoa mix and the marshmallows, making it easy to distribute the ingredients.

PREP TIME: 15 MINUTES • BAKE TIME: 35 MINUTES • YIELD: 9 SERVINGS

¾ cup granulated sugar

½ cup (1 stick) unsalted butter, at room temperature

1 teaspoon vanilla extract

2 large eggs

1 cup all-purpose flour

¼ cup unsweetened cocoa powder

1 teaspoon baking powder

1 teaspoon baking soda

2 tablespoons hot water

4 envelopes (0.73-ounce packets) hot cocoa mix, without marshmallows

½ cup marshmallow bits

1. Preheat the oven to 350°F. Coat an 8-inch square baking pan with nonstick baking spray with flour.

2. In a large bowl, using an electric mixer on medium speed, cream the sugar and butter together until creamy. Beat in the vanilla, then add the eggs, one at a time, beating just until each egg is incorporated.

3. In a medium bowl, combine the flour, cocoa, baking powder, and baking soda.

4. Add the hot water to a coffee cup. Microwave for 30 seconds. Pour all the hot cocoa mix in the coffee cup and stir until dissolved. Add the hot cocoa mixture and dry ingredients to the butter-sugar mixture in the large bowl, alternating back and forth between the two, starting and ending with the flour mixture and beating on medium speed. Scrape down the sides and bottom of the bowl with a spatula and stir in any unmixed bits of batter. Fold in the marshmallow bits.

5. Pour the batter into the prepared baking pan. Bake until a toothpick inserted in the center comes out clean, 30 to 35 minutes.

6. Let the cake cool completely before removing it from the pan. Once cooled, cut into three strips lengthwise and three strips widthwise for 9 servings.

STORAGE: Will keep tightly covered with plastic wrap or in an airtight container at room temperature for 4 to 5 days.

TOP IT OFF: As a fun addition, top the cake with a layer of mini marshmallows about 5 minutes before the cake is done baking and let them brown up. Sprinkle a very light dusting of hot cocoa mix on top of the marshmallows.

BLUEBERRY-LEMON SNACK CAKE

This tastes like summer in a cake—it's sweet, tart, and incredibly fruity.
Frozen berries are fine to use, so this can be made year-round.

PREP TIME: 15 MINUTES • BAKE TIME: 40 MINUTES • YIELD: 9 SERVINGS

1 cup granulated sugar

¾ cup (1½ sticks)
unsalted butter, melted

¼ cup fresh lemon juice

1 tablespoon grated
lemon zest

2 large eggs

1 cup all-purpose flour

1 teaspoon
baking powder

⅛ teaspoon salt

½ cup frozen or
fresh blueberries

1. Preheat the oven to 350°F. Coat an 8-inch square baking pan with nonstick baking spray with flour.

2. In a medium bowl, using an electric mixer on medium speed, cream the sugar and butter together until combined. Beat in the lemon juice and zest, and eggs until well combined.

3. In a large bowl, combine the flour, baking powder, and salt. Add the lemon mixture and beat on medium speed, just until the flour is worked into the batter. Fold in the blueberries.

4. Pour the batter into the prepared baking pan. Bake until a toothpick inserted in the center comes out clean, 35 to 40 minutes.

5. Let the cake cool completely before removing it from the pan. Cut into three strips lengthwise and three strips widthwise for 9 servings.

STORAGE: Will keep tightly covered with plastic wrap or in an airtight container at room temperature for 4 to 5 days.

TIP: Any frozen blueberries will work in this recipe but I recommend the smaller wild blueberries. Wild blueberries aren't as juicy as regular blueberries, so they don't turn the cake purple. They are also sweeter than regular blueberries.

CHERRY ALMOND SNACK CAKE

This has plenty of fresh cherries, with lots of sliced almonds baked on top to complete the look and taste. A cherry pitter will come in handy for this recipe, but the cherries can easily be cut in half and pitted.

PREP TIME: 15 MINUTES • BAKE TIME: 35 MINUTES • YIELD: 9 SERVINGS

¾ cup granulated sugar

½ cup (1 stick) unsalted butter, room temperature

1 teaspoon vanilla extract

¼ teaspoon almond extract

2 large eggs

1½ cups all-purpose flour

1 teaspoon baking powder

1 teaspoon baking soda

⅛ teaspoon salt

½ cup evaporated milk, whole milk, or buttermilk

¾ cup fresh cherries, stemmed, pitted, and halved

¼ cup sliced almonds

1. Preheat the oven to 350°F. Coat an 8-inch square baking pan with nonstick baking spray with flour.

2. In a large bowl, using an electric mixer on medium speed, cream the sugar and butter together until creamy. Beat in the vanilla and almond extract, then add the eggs, one at a time, beating just until each egg is incorporated.

3. In a medium bowl, combine the flour, baking powder, baking soda, and salt. Add the dry ingredients and evaporated milk to the large bowl, alternating back and forth between the two, starting and ending with flour and beating on medium speed. Scrape down the sides and bottom of the bowl with a spatula and stir in any unmixed bits of batter.

4. Pour the batter into the prepared baking pan. Gently push the cherries into the batter, then sprinkle the almonds on top. Bake until a toothpick inserted into the center comes out clean, 30 to 35 minutes.

5. Let the cake cool completely before removing it from the pan. Once cooled, cut into three strips lengthwise and three strips widthwise for 9 servings.

STORAGE: Will keep tightly covered with plastic wrap or in an airtight container at room temperature for 4 to 5 days.

MARBLED LOAF CAKE

If you can't decide whether you like vanilla or chocolate cake more, this marbled loaf cake gives you both in a single slice. Serve with a scoop of ice cream for a cool summer dessert.

PREP TIME: 15 MINUTES • BAKE TIME: 1 HOUR 5 MINUTES • YIELD: 12 SERVINGS

1¼ cups
granulated sugar

½ cup (1 stick)
unsalted butter, at
room temperature

½ cup full-fat sour cream

2 teaspoons
vanilla extract

2 large eggs

1¾ cups all-purpose flour

1 teaspoon
baking powder

½ teaspoon baking soda

¼ teaspoon salt

¼ cup whole milk

2 tablespoons
unsweetened
cocoa powder

1. Preheat the oven to 350°F. Line an 8½-by-4½-inch loaf pan with heavy-duty aluminum foil or parchment paper. Coat the foil or parchment with nonstick baking spray. Set aside.

2. In a large bowl, using an electric mixer on medium speed, cream the sugar and butter together until combined. Beat in the sour cream, vanilla, and eggs just until the eggs are incorporated.

3. In a medium bowl, combine the flour, baking powder, baking soda, and salt. Add the dry ingredients and the milk to the butter-sugar mixture in the large bowl, alternating back and forth between the two, starting and ending with the flour mixture and beating on medium speed. Scrape down the sides and bottom of the bowl with a spatula and stir in any unmixed bits of batter.

4. Transfer about 1 cup of the batter to a small bowl. Stir in the cocoa until completely combined.

CONTINUED ▶

MARBLED LOAF CAKE

continued

5. Pour half the vanilla batter in the prepared loaf pan. Pour half the chocolate batter on top of the vanilla batter. Repeat with the remaining halves of the vanilla and chocolate batters. With a butter knife or skewer, swirl the batters together, taking care not to mix them too much. Bake until a toothpick inserted into the center comes out clean, 60 to 65 minutes.

6. Let the cake cool completely, then turn out onto a serving plate. Cut and serve.

STORAGE: Will keep tightly covered with plastic wrap or in an airtight container at room temperature for 4 to 5 days.

TOP IT OFF: Depending on whether you are a vanilla or chocolate fan, you can drizzle it with Chocolate Ganache (page 126), Vanilla Glaze (page 128), or both!

OATMEAL SNACK CAKE

This maple cinnamon oatmeal cake is incredibly light and fluffy.

PREP TIME: 15 MINUTES • BAKE TIME: 45 MINUTES • YIELD: 9 SERVINGS

1 cup quick-cooking oats

1 cup boiling water

½ cup (1 stick) unsalted butter, at room temperature

½ cup granulated sugar

½ cup packed light brown sugar

2 teaspoons vanilla extract

1 teaspoon maple extract

2 large eggs

1 cup all-purpose flour

1 teaspoon baking soda

½ teaspoon ground cinnamon

⅛ teaspoon ground nutmeg

¼ teaspoon salt

1. Preheat the oven to 350°F. Coat an 8-inch square baking pan with nonstick baking spray with flour.

2. Add the oats to the boiling water and stir until the water is mostly absorbed. Set aside.

3. In a medium bowl, using an electric mixer on medium speed, cream the butter and granulated and brown sugars together until light and fluffy. Beat in the vanilla and maple extract, then add the eggs, one at a time, beating just until each egg is incorporated.

4. In a large bowl, combine the flour, baking soda, cinnamon, nutmeg, and salt. Add the butter mixture and beat on medium speed, just until the flour is worked into the batter. Add the oatmeal and beat until evenly distributed in the batter.

5. Pour the batter into the prepared baking pan. Bake until a toothpick inserted into the center comes out clean, 40 to 45 minutes.

6. Let the cake cool completely before removing it from the pan. Cut into three strips lengthwise and three strips widthwise for 9 servings.

STORAGE: Will keep tightly covered with plastic wrap or in an airtight container at room temperature for 4 to 5 days.

TOP IT OFF: For extra maple flavor, drizzle the cooled cake with Maple Glaze (page 128).

CRANBERRY-GINGER SNACK CAKE

A wonderful cake for winter, with the tart, spicy kick of cranberries and fresh ginger. I call for dried cranberries but you can swap in fresh cranberries when they're in season.

PREP TIME: 15 MINUTES • BAKE TIME: 35 MINUTES • YIELD: 9 SERVINGS

¾ cup (1½ sticks) unsalted butter, melted

1 cup granulated sugar

1 teaspoon vanilla extract

1 teaspoon finely grated peeled fresh ginger

¼ cup whole milk

2 large eggs

1 cup all-purpose flour

1 teaspoon baking powder

⅛ teaspoon salt

½ cup dried cranberries

1. Preheat the oven to 350°F. Coat an 8-inch square baking pan with nonstick baking spray with flour.

2. In a large bowl, using an electric mixer on medium speed, cream the butter and sugar together until combined. Beat in the vanilla, ginger, milk, and eggs until the eggs are worked into the batter.

3. In a medium bowl, combine the flour, baking powder, and salt. Add to the butter mixture and beat on medium speed, just until the flour is worked into the batter. Fold in the cranberries.

4. Pour the batter into the prepared baking pan. Bake until a toothpick inserted into the center comes out clean, 30 to 35 minutes.

5. Let the cake cool completely before removing it from the pan. Once cooled, cut into three strips lengthwise and three strips widthwise for 9 servings.

STORAGE: Will keep tightly covered with plastic wrap or in an airtight container at room temperature for 4 to 5 days.

VARIATION: Substitute dried blueberries, dried cherries, (or any other dried fruit that would pair well with ginger) for the cranberries.

RASPBERRY WHITE CHOCOLATE LOAF CAKE

This loaf cake is one of my favorites. Its sweetness comes from the chunks of white chocolate and raspberries scattered throughout.

PREP TIME: 10 MINUTES • BAKE TIME: 1 HOUR 5 MINUTES • YIELD: 12 SLICES

1¼ cups granulated sugar

½ cup (1 stick) unsalted butter, at room temperature

½ cup full-fat sour cream

2 teaspoons vanilla extract

2 large eggs

1¾ cups all-purpose flour

1 teaspoon baking powder

½ teaspoon baking soda

¼ teaspoon salt

¼ cup whole milk

1 cup frozen or fresh raspberries

½ cup white chocolate chips

1. Preheat the oven to 350°F. Line an 8½-by-4½-inch loaf pan with heavy-duty aluminum foil or parchment paper. Coat with nonstick baking spray.

2. In a large bowl, using an electric mixer on medium speed, cream the sugar and butter together until light and fluffy. Beat in the sour cream, vanilla, and eggs just until incorporated.

3. In a medium bowl, combine the flour, baking powder, baking soda, and salt. Add the dry ingredients and milk to the butter-sugar mixture in the large bowl, in multiple additions, alternating back and forth between the two, starting and ending with the flour mixture and beating on medium speed. Scrape down the bowl and stir in any unmixed bits of batter. Fold in the raspberries and chocolate chips.

4. Pour the batter into the prepared loaf pan. Bake until a toothpick inserted into the center comes out clean, 60 to 65 minutes.

5. Let the cake cool completely, then turn out onto a serving plate. Cut and serve.

STORAGE: Will keep tightly covered with plastic wrap or in an airtight container at room temperature for 4 to 5 days.

TOP IT OFF: White Chocolate Ganache (page 126) would make the perfect drizzle for this loaf cake.

ORANGE CREAMSICLE LOAF CAKE

Loaded with orange juice, orange zest, and orange extract, this is the cake version of that beloved ice cream bar. For added measure, white chocolate chips are sprinkled in the cake, too.

PREP TIME: 15 MINUTES • BAKE TIME: 1 HOUR 25 MINUTES • YIELD: 12 SERVINGS

1 cup granulated sugar

½ cup (1 stick) unsalted butter, room temperature

½ cup full-fat sour cream

2 teaspoons vanilla extract

2 teaspoons orange extract

1 tablespoon grated orange zest

2 large eggs

1¾ cups all-purpose flour

1 teaspoon baking powder

½ teaspoon baking soda

¼ teaspoon salt

¼ cup pulp-free orange juice

Orange gel food coloring (optional)

1 cup white chocolate chips

1. Preheat the oven to 350°F. Line an 8½-by-4½-inch loaf pan with heavy-duty aluminum foil or parchment paper. Coat the foil or parchment with nonstick baking spray. Set aside.

2. In a large bowl, using an electric mixer on medium speed, cream the sugar and butter together until light and fluffy. Beat in the sour cream, vanilla, orange extract and zest, and eggs, beating just until the eggs are incorporated.

3. In a medium bowl, combine the flour, baking powder, baking soda, and salt. Add the dry ingredients and orange juice (with the food coloring added to it, if using) to the butter-sugar mixture in the large bowl in multiple additions, alternating back and forth between the two, starting and ending with the flour mixture and beating on medium speed. Scrape down the sides and bottom of the bowl with a spatula and stir in any unmixed bits of batter. Fold the white chocolate chips into the batter.

4. Pour the batter into the prepared loaf pan. Bake until a toothpick inserted into the center comes out clean, 80 to 85 minutes.

5. Let the cake cool completely, then turn out onto a serving plate. Cut and serve.

STORAGE: Will keep tightly covered with plastic wrap or in an airtight container at room temperature for 4 to 5 days.

TOP IT OFF: This loaf cake has plenty of orange flavor, but if you want more, drizzle it with White Chocolate Ganache (page 126) with 1 teaspoon grated orange zest stirred in.

CHOCOLATE-STRAWBERRY ICE CREAM SNACK CAKE

Ice cream and cake make a great pair. This combo has a rich chocolate base, topped with an oh-so-easy-to-make-from-scratch ice cream made with fresh strawberries.

PREP TIME: 20 MINUTES • BAKE TIME: 25 MINUTES • YIELD: 9 SERVINGS

FOR THE CAKE

⅓ cup boiling water

¼ cup vegetable oil

⅓ cup full-fat sour cream

¼ cup unsweetened cocoa powder

1 teaspoon vanilla extract

1 large egg

¾ cup granulated sugar

½ cup all-purpose flour

½ teaspoon baking powder

½ teaspoon baking soda

¼ teaspoon salt

1. Preheat the oven to 350°F. Coat an 8-inch square baking pan with nonstick baking spray with flour.

2. For the cake, in a medium bowl, whisk the boiling water, oil, sour cream, cocoa, and vanilla together until the cocoa and sour cream are fully combined. It will be thick and creamy. Whisk in the egg.

3. In a large bowl, combine the sugar, flour, baking powder, baking soda, and salt. Add the cocoa mixture and whisk until smooth.

4. Pour the batter into the prepared baking pan. Bake until a toothpick inserted into the center comes out clean, 20 to 25 minutes. Let cool completely.

FOR THE ICE CREAM

1 cup heavy cream

½ (14-ounce) can sweetened condensed milk

½ cup hulled and finely chopped strawberries (5 to 7 strawberries)

1 teaspoon vanilla extract

5. For the ice cream, in a large bowl, using an electric mixer on medium speed, beat the cream until soft peaks form. Turn the mixer on high and beat until firm peaks form. (When you pull your beater out of the whipped cream, it should form a peak and hold its shape without falling over.) Fold in the condensed milk, strawberries, and vanilla until incorporated. Pour the strawberry ice cream on top of the cooled cake and place in the freezer until the ice cream is firm, 3 to 4 hours. Cut into three strips lengthwise and three strips widthwise for 9 servings.

STORAGE: Will keep tightly covered with plastic wrap or in an airtight container in the freezer for 4 to 5 days.

VARIATION: Substitute finely chopped maraschino cherries, fresh blackberries, or fresh raspberries for the strawberries.

Pineapple Upside-Down
Skillet Cake, page 88

SKILLET CAKES

I love that skillet cakes can be baked and served right from their pan. They have a rustic feel to them, don't require a cake plate, and don't need to be slathered in frosting. But if you do desire some frosting, I provide delectable suggestions in some of the recipes. This chapter has something for everyone: caramelized upside-down skillet cakes, tangy fruit cakes, decadent chocolate cakes, and even a blueberry cornmeal cake.

PINEAPPLE UPSIDE-DOWN SKILLET CAKE

This has perfectly caramelized pineapple rings, with a maraschino cherry peeking out of the center of each. It comes together quickly and has a beautiful presentation.

PREP TIME: 15 MINUTES • BAKE TIME: 1 HOUR • YIELD: 8 SERVINGS

FOR THE TOPPING

6 tablespoons (¾ stick) unsalted butter, melted

¾ cup packed light brown sugar

7 pineapple rings (reserve the juice)

7 maraschino cherries

FOR THE CAKE

1¼ cups granulated sugar

10 tablespoons (1¼ sticks) unsalted butter, at room temperature

1 teaspoon vanilla extract

2 large eggs

2 cups all-purpose flour

1. Preheat the oven to 350°F. Line a 10-inch skillet with aluminum foil. Coat with nonstick baking spray with flour.

2. For the topping, put the butter in the prepared skillet and put the skillet in the oven until the butter is completely melted, about 5 minutes. Remove the skillet from the oven and immediately add the brown sugar. Using a spatula, stir the brown sugar and butter until combined. Arrange the pineapple rings in a single layer in the bottom of the skillet. Place a maraschino cherry in the center of each pineapple ring. Set the skillet aside.

3. For the cake, in a large bowl, using an electric mixer on medium speed, cream the sugar and butter together until light and fluffy. Beat in the vanilla, then add the eggs one at a time, beating just until each egg is incorporated. Scrape down the sides and bottom of the bowl with a spatula.

4. In a medium bowl, whisk together the flour, baking powder, and salt. Stir the pineapple juice into the buttermilk. Add the dry ingredients and buttermilk mixture to the butter-sugar mixture in the large bowl, alternating back and forth between the two, starting and ending with the flour mixture and beating on medium speed. Scrape down the sides and

1 tablespoon
baking powder

½ teaspoon salt

¼ cup pineapple juice,
reserved from the can

½ cup buttermilk

bottom of the bowl with a spatula and stir in any unmixed bits of batter.

5. Dollop all of the batter on top of the pineapple rings. Gently spread the batter out using the spatula. Bake until a toothpick inserted into the center comes out clean, about 1 hour.

6. Let cool 5 minutes. Place a serving platter facedown on the skillet and flip the skillet over to catch the cake. Pull the foil away from the sides of the skillet and then away from the sides of the cake. Let the cake cool to room temperature before serving it.

STORAGE: Will keep tightly covered with plastic wrap or in an airtight container at room temperature for 3 to 4 days.

VARIATION: Sprinkle ¼ cup pecans around the pineapple rings after placing the maraschino cherries.

TEXAS CHOCOLATE SKILLET CAKE

This is one of the few cakes in this book with a glaze, and it's worth the extra effort. The cake and glaze can both be whipped up quickly, which is always great for last-minute gatherings.

PREP TIME: 20 MINUTES • BAKE TIME: 50 MINUTES • YIELD: 8 SERVINGS

FOR THE CAKE

¾ cup (1½ sticks) unsalted butter, melted

½ cup water

2 cups granulated sugar

½ cup buttermilk

½ cup full-fat sour cream

¼ cup vegetable oil

¼ cup unsweetened cocoa powder

1 teaspoon vanilla extract

2 large eggs, lightly beaten

2 cups all-purpose flour

1 teaspoon baking soda

¼ teaspoon salt

1. Preheat the oven to 350°F. Coat a 10-inch skillet with nonstick baking spray with flour.

2. For the cake, in a medium microwave-safe bowl, microwave the butter and water on high for 1½ to 2 minutes, until the water is boiling. Add the sugar, buttermilk, sour cream, oil, and cocoa, and whisk until creamy. Whisk in the vanilla and eggs just until the eggs are worked into the batter.

3. In a large bowl, combine the flour, baking soda, and salt. Add the cocoa mixture and whisk until the batter is smooth.

4. Pour the batter into the prepared skillet. Bake until a toothpick inserted into the center comes out clean, about 50 minutes.

5. Let cake cool for 10 minutes while you make the glaze.

FOR THE GLAZE

¼ cup (½ stick)
unsalted butter

2½ tablespoons
whole milk

1¼ tablespoons
unsweetened
cocoa powder

1¾ cups powdered sugar

¼ teaspoon salt

⅓ cup chopped pecans

6. For the glaze, in a medium saucepan over medium heat, whisk the butter, milk, and cocoa together until smooth. When the glaze comes to a boil, remove the pan from the heat and whisk in the powdered sugar and salt until the glaze is smooth. Stir in the pecans. Pour the glaze over the cake while it is still warm. Let cool for 10 minutes before serving from the skillet.

STORAGE: Will keep tightly covered with plastic wrap or in an airtight container at room temperature for 3 to 4 days.

TOP IT OFF: Take it to the limit with a scoop of vanilla ice cream.

STRAWBERRY SKILLET CAKE

This cake is moist and tender from the buttermilk and chock full of strawberries.

PREP TIME: 15 MINUTES • BAKE TIME: 55 MINUTES • YIELD: 8 SERVINGS

1 cup granulated sugar

½ cup (1 stick) unsalted butter, at room temperature

2 teaspoons vanilla extract

2 large eggs

1½ cups all-purpose flour

1 teaspoon baking powder

¼ teaspoon salt

½ cup buttermilk

2¾ cups sliced fresh strawberries (about 15 to 20 strawberries)

1. Preheat the oven to 350°F. Spray a 10-inch skillet with nonstick baking spray with flour.

2. In a large bowl, using an electric mixer on medium speed, cream the sugar and butter together until light and fluffy. Beat in the vanilla, then add the eggs, one at a time, beating just until each egg is incorporated. Scrape down the sides and bottom of the bowl with a spatula.

3. In a medium bowl, sift together the flour, baking powder, and salt. Add the dry ingredients and buttermilk to the butter-sugar mixture in the large bowl, alternating back and forth between the two, starting and ending with the flour mixture and beating on medium speed. Scrape down the sides and bottom of the bowl with a spatula and stir in any unmixed bits of batter. Fold in the strawberries.

4. Pour the batter into the prepared skillet. Spread the batter out with a spatula. Bake until a toothpick inserted into the center comes out clean, 50 to 55 minutes. Let cool completely before serving.

STORAGE: Will keep tightly covered with plastic wrap or in an airtight container at room temperature for up to 2 days.

TOP IT OFF: This cake is perfect with a dollop of homemade Whipped Cream (page 130).

LEMON OLIVE OIL SKILLET CAKE

This light and fluffy cake packs a serious punch of lemon. The recipe uses a light-tasting olive oil, but feel free to use your favorite olive oil.

PREP TIME: 15 MINUTES • BAKE TIME: 45 MINUTES • YIELD: 8 SERVINGS

1 cup granulated sugar

½ cup light-tasting or extra-virgin olive oil

¼ cup buttermilk

¼ cup fresh lemon juice

1 tablespoon grated lemon zest

1 teaspoon vanilla extract

½ teaspoon lemon extract

2 large eggs, lightly beaten

1½ cups all-purpose flour

½ teaspoon baking powder

½ teaspoon baking soda

¼ teaspoon salt

1. Preheat the oven to 350°F. Coat a 10-inch skillet with nonstick baking spray with flour.

2. In a medium bowl, whisk the sugar, oil, buttermilk, lemon juice and zest, vanilla, lemon extract, and eggs together until well combined.

3. In a large bowl, whisk together the flour, baking powder, baking soda, and salt. Add the buttermilk mixture. Using an electric mixer on medium speed, beat just until the flour is worked in. The batter will be runny.

4. Pour the batter into the prepared skillet. Bake until a toothpick inserted into the center comes out clean, 40 to 45 minutes. Let cool completely before serving.

STORAGE: Will keep tightly covered with plastic wrap or in an airtight container at room temperature for 4 to 5 days.

TOP IT OFF: This is so pretty dusted with powdered sugar or drizzled with Lemon Glaze (page 128).

BANANA UPSIDE-DOWN SKILLET CAKE

This moist cake is topped with slices of caramelized bananas
and has a hint of cinnamon.

PREP TIME: 20 MINUTES • BAKE TIME: 60 MINUTES • YIELD: 8 SERVINGS

FOR THE TOPPING

6 tablespoons (¾ stick)
unsalted butter, melted

¾ cup packed light
brown sugar

2 bananas, sliced

FOR THE CAKE

½ cup (1 stick)
unsalted butter,
room temperature

¾ cup granulated sugar

¼ cup packed light
brown sugar

2 overripe
bananas, mashed

¼ cup full-fat sour cream

1 teaspoon
vanilla extract

1 large egg

1. Preheat the oven to 350°F. Line a 10-inch skillet
   with aluminum foil. Coat with nonstick baking spray
   with flour.

2. For the topping, put the butter in the prepared skillet and put the skillet in the oven until the butter is
   completely melted, about 5 minutes. Remove the
   skillet from the oven, immediately add the brown
   sugar and, using a spatula, stir the sugar and butter
   together until combined. Arrange the banana slices
   in a single layer on top of the brown sugar mixture.
   Set the skillet aside.

3. For the cake, in a large bowl, using an electric mixer
   on medium speed, cream the butter and granulated
   and brown sugars together until light and fluffy. Beat
   in the bananas, sour cream, and vanilla. Beat in the
   egg. Scrape down the sides and bottom of the bowl
   with a spatula.

4. In a medium bowl, sift together the flour, baking
   soda, salt, and cinnamon. Add the dry ingredients
   and buttermilk to the butter-sugar mixture in the
   large bowl, alternating back and forth between the
   two, starting and ending with the flour mixture and
   beating on medium speed. Scrape down the sides
   and bottom of the bowl with a spatula and stir in
   any unmixed bits of batter.

2 cups all-purpose flour

1 teaspoon baking soda

½ teaspoon salt

½ teaspoon
ground cinnamon

½ cup buttermilk

5. Dollop all of the batter on top of the banana slices. Gently spread the batter out using the spatula. Bake until a toothpick inserted into the center comes out clean, 55 to 60 minutes.

6. Let cool 5 minutes. Place a serving platter facedown over the skillet and flip the skillet over to catch the cake. Pull the foil away from the sides of the skillet and then away from the sides of the cake.

7. Let the cake cool to room temperature before serving it.

STORAGE: Will keep tightly covered with plastic wrap or in an airtight container at room temperature for 3 to 4 days.

VARIATION: Switch out half of the sliced bananas for sliced strawberries to make a Strawberry-Banana Upside-Down Skillet Cake.

CHOCOLATE LAVA SKILLET CAKE

This gooey chocolate cake is perfectly divine. The lava is at the bottom of the skillet and flows out when the cake is cut.

PREP TIME: 15 MINUTES • BAKE TIME: 20 MINUTES • YIELD: 8 SERVINGS

1 cup milk
chocolate chips

½ cup heavy cream

¼ cup (½ stick)
unsalted butter

2 teaspoons
vanilla extract

3 large eggs,
lightly beaten

6 tablespoons
granulated
sugar, divided

4 tablespoons
unsweetened cocoa
powder, divided

1 cup all-purpose flour

1 teaspoon
baking powder

¼ teaspoon salt

½ cup packed light
brown sugar

½ cup hot strongly
brewed coffee

1. Preheat the oven to 350°F. Coat a 10-inch skillet with nonstick baking spray with flour.

2. In a medium microwave-safe bowl, microwave the chocolate chips, cream, and butter in 30-second intervals, stirring after each interval, until the chips and butter are melted and the mixture is smooth. Whisk in the vanilla and eggs until incorporated.

3. In a large bowl, combine 4 tablespoons of the granulated sugar, 2 tablespoons of the cocoa, the flour, baking powder, and salt. Add the chocolate mixture in and beat with an electric mixer on medium speed until smooth. Pour the batter into the prepared skillet. Evenly spread the batter out.

4. In a small bowl, whisk together the remaining 2 tablespoons of granulated sugar and the remaining 2 tablespoons of cocoa, the brown sugar, and coffee until the cocoa is incorporated. Pour the coffee mixture on top of the cake batter. Bake until the cake is jiggly when gently shaken, but the top is dry and crispy, 17 to 20 minutes. Let cool to room temperature before scooping the cake in a serving dish.

STORAGE: Will keep tightly covered with plastic wrap or in an airtight container at room temperature for 3 to 4 days.

TOP IT OFF: A scoop of vanilla ice cream is a natural partner for this, as is homemade Whipped Cream (page 130).

CHERRY ALMOND SKILLET CAKE

This cake is packed with fresh cherries and almond flavor.
The sliced almond topping toasts up perfectly in the oven
while the cake is baking.

PREP TIME: 15 MINUTES • BAKE TIME: 59 MINUTES • YIELD: 8 SERVINGS

1¼ cups plus
½ tablespoon granulated
sugar, divided

¾ cup (1½ sticks)
unsalted butter, at
room temperature

½ cup full-fat sour cream

1 teaspoon
vanilla extract

1 teaspoon
almond extract

3 large eggs

1¾ cups all-purpose flour

1 teaspoon
baking powder

½ teaspoon baking soda

¼ teaspoon salt

1 cup fresh cherries,
stemmed, pitted,
and halved

½ cup sliced almonds

1. Preheat the oven to 350°F. Coat a 10-inch skillet with nonstick baking spray with flour.

2. In a large bowl, using an electric mixer on medium speed, cream together 1¼ cups of the sugar with the butter until light and fluffy. Beat in the sour cream, vanilla, and almond extract, then add the eggs, one at a time, beating just until each egg is incorporated. Scrape down the bowl with a spatula.

3. In a medium bowl, sift together the flour, baking powder, baking soda, and salt. Add the dry ingredients to the butter-sugar mixture in the large bowl and beat on medium speed, just until the flour is incorporated. Scrape down the sides and bottom of the bowl with a spatula and stir in any unmixed bits of batter. Fold in the cherries.

4. Pour the batter into the prepared skillet. Spread the batter out with a spatula. Sprinkle the top of the cake batter with the remaining ½ tablespoon sugar and the almonds. Bake until a toothpick inserted into the center comes out clean, 54 to 59 minutes. Let cool before slicing and serving out of the pan.

STORAGE: Will keep tightly covered with plastic wrap or in an airtight container at room temperature for 3 to 4 days.

TOP IT OFF: Dust the cooled cake with powdered sugar.

PEANUT BUTTER CHOCOLATE CHIP SKILLET CAKE

This has the perfect balance of nutty and sweet. It's dense, moist, and delicious. I love to sprinkle the chocolate chips on top just before baking so some rest on top of the finished cake.

PREP TIME: 15 MINUTES • BAKE TIME: 49 MINUTES • YIELD: 8 SERVINGS

¾ cup water

½ cup (1 stick) unsalted butter, cubed

¾ cup full-fat sour cream

½ cup creamy peanut butter

1½ tablespoons vegetable oil

1 teaspoon vanilla extract

2 large eggs, lightly beaten

1½ cups all-purpose flour

½ cup granulated sugar

½ cup packed light brown sugar

¼ teaspoon baking powder

1 teaspoon baking soda

¼ teaspoon salt

1 cup semisweet chocolate chips

1. Preheat the oven to 350°F. Coat a 10-inch skillet with nonstick baking spray with flour.

2. In a medium microwave-safe bowl, microwave the water and butter on high for 1½ to 2 minutes, until the water is boiling. Add the sour cream, peanut butter, oil, and vanilla, and whisk together until creamy. Whisk in the eggs just until combined.

3. In a large bowl, combine the flour, granulated and brown sugars, baking powder, baking soda, and salt. Add the peanut butter mixture and whisk until the batter is smooth.

4. Pour the batter into the prepared skillet. Sprinkle the chocolate chips on top. Bake until a toothpick inserted into the center comes out clean, 44 to 49 minutes.

5. Let cool completely before slicing and serving from the pan.

STORAGE: Will keep tightly covered with plastic wrap or in an airtight container at room temperature for 4 to 5 days.

TOP IT OFF: Peanut Butter Glaze (page 129) is the perfect finish for this.

TURTLE SKILLET CAKE

Have you ever had the chocolates that resemble a turtle
made from pecans, caramel, and chocolate? This is a skillet cake version:
a flourless cake topped with caramel and pecans. It's rich, decadent,
and just the treat for any chocolate lover.

PREP TIME: 20 MINUTES • BAKE TIME: 25 MINUTES • YIELD: 8 SERVINGS

¾ cup milk
chocolate chips

6 tablespoons (¾ stick)
unsalted butter, cubed

½ cup plus
2 tablespoons
granulated sugar

1 teaspoon
vanilla extract

3 large eggs,
lightly beaten

6 tablespoons
unsweetened
cocoa powder

½ teaspoon salt

1 cup diced caramel
squares (20 pieces)

1 cup pecan pieces

1. Preheat the oven to 375°F. Coat a 10-inch skillet with nonstick baking spray with flour.

2. In a medium microwave-safe bowl, microwave the chocolate chips and butter in 30-second intervals, stirring after each until the chocolate chips and butter are completely melted and the mixture is smooth. Whisk in the sugar, vanilla, and eggs. Whisk in the cocoa and salt until the batter is smooth.

3. Pour the batter into the prepared skillet. Spread the batter out with a spatula. Sprinkle the caramels and pecans on top of the batter. Bake until a toothpick inserted into the center comes out clean, 20 to 25 minutes.

4. Let cool before slicing and serving out of the pan.

STORAGE: Will keep tightly covered with plastic wrap or in an airtight container at room temperature for 4 to 5 days.

TOP IT OFF: For an over-the-top turtle skillet cake, drizzle warm store-bought caramel sauce on top of the cake just before serving.

PECAN UPSIDE-DOWN SKILLET CAKE

Is there anything better than a pecan coated in brown sugar?
This cake is loaded with pecans caramelized in a brown sugar syrup.

PREP TIME: 15 MINUTES • BAKE TIME: 56 MINUTES • YIELD: 8 SERVINGS

FOR THE TOPPING

6 tablespoons (¾ stick)
unsalted butter, at
room temperature

¾ cup packed light
brown sugar

1 cup pecan halves

FOR THE CAKE

1¼ cups
granulated sugar

10 tablespoons
(1¼ sticks)
unsalted butter, at
room temperature

1 teaspoon
vanilla extract

2 large eggs

2 cups all-purpose flour

1 tablespoon
baking powder

½ teaspoon salt

¾ cup buttermilk

1. Preheat the oven to 350°F. Line a 10-inch skillet with aluminum foil. Coat with nonstick baking spray.

2. For the topping, add the butter to the prepared skillet and put in the oven until the butter is completely melted, about 5 minutes. Remove the skillet from the oven, immediately add the brown sugar, and, using a spatula, stir the sugar and butter together until combined. Sprinkle the pecans over the mixture as evenly as possible. Set the skillet aside while preparing the cake.

3. For the cake, in a large bowl, using an electric mixer on medium speed, cream the sugar and butter together until light and fluffy. Beat in the vanilla, then add the eggs, one at a time, beating just until each egg is incorporated. Scrape down the sides and bottom of the bowl with a spatula.

4. In medium bowl, sift together the flour, baking powder, and salt. Add the dry ingredients and buttermilk to the butter-sugar mixture in the large bowl, alternating back and forth between the two, starting and ending with the flour mixture and beating on medium speed. Scrape down the sides and bottom of the bowl and stir in any unmixed bits of batter with a spatula.

5. Dollop all the batter on top of the brown sugar–pecan mixture. Gently spread the batter out using the spatula. Bake until a toothpick inserted into the center comes out clean, 51 to 56 minutes.

6. Let cool 5 minutes. Place a serving platter facedown over the skillet and flip the skillet over to catch the cake. Pull the foil away from the sides of the skillet and then away from the sides of the cake. Let the cake cool to room temperature before slicing and serving it.

STORAGE: Will keep tightly covered with plastic wrap or in an airtight container at room temperature for 3 to 4 days.

VARIATION: Swap out the pecans for walnut halves, slivered or sliced almonds, or chopped hazelnuts.

CINNAMON ROLL SKILLET CAKE

Enjoy this for breakfast *and* dessert.

PREP TIME: 15 MINUTES • BAKE TIME: 38 MINUTES • YIELD: 8 SERVINGS

FOR THE TOPPING

½ cup packed light
brown sugar

¼ cup (½ stick) unsalted
butter, melted

2 tablespoons
all-purpose flour

1 tablespoon
ground cinnamon

FOR THE CAKE

¾ cup granulated sugar

10 tablespoons
(1¼ sticks)
unsalted butter, at
room temperature

2 teaspoons
vanilla extract

1 large egg

1½ cups all-purpose flour

1½ teaspoons
baking powder

½ teaspoon salt

½ cup buttermilk

1. Preheat the oven to 350°F. Coat a 10-inch skillet with nonstick baking spray with flour.

2. For the topping, in a small bowl, stir together the sugar, melted butter, flour, and cinnamon until well combined.

3. For the cake, in a large bowl, using an electric mixer on medium speed, cream the sugar and butter together until light and fluffy. Beat in the vanilla and egg until the egg is incorporated. Scrape down the sides and bottom of the bowl with a spatula.

4. In a medium bowl, sift together the flour, baking powder, and salt. Add the dry ingredients and buttermilk to the butter-sugar mixture in the large bowl, alternating back and forth between the two, starting and ending with the flour mixture and beating on medium speed. Scrape down the sides and bottom of the bowl with a spatula.

5. Pour the batter into the prepared skillet. Spread the batter out with a spatula. Spoon the topping over the batter. With a skewer or toothpick, swirl the topping into the batter. Bake until a toothpick inserted into the center comes out clean, 33 to 38 minutes. Let cool before slicing and serving from the pan.

STORAGE: Will keep tightly covered with plastic wrap or in an airtight container at room temperature for 4 to 5 days.

TOP IT OFF: Drizzle with Cream Cheese Glaze (page 127).

PEACH SPICE SKILLET CAKE

This cake reminds me of the beginning of fall. The cinnamon and nutmeg add spice perfectly and the peaches keep it incredibly moist.

PREP TIME: 15 MINUTES • BAKE TIME: 45 MINUTES • YIELD: 8 SERVINGS

10 tablespoons (1¼ sticks) unsalted butter, at room temperature

½ cup packed light brown sugar

¼ cup granulated sugar

2 teaspoons vanilla extract

1 large egg

1½ cups all-purpose flour

1½ teaspoons baking powder

½ teaspoon salt

½ teaspoon ground cinnamon

⅛ teaspoon ground nutmeg

½ cup buttermilk

1¼ cups diced peaches

1. Preheat the oven to 350°F. Coat a 10-inch skillet with nonstick baking spray with flour.

2. In a large bowl, using an electric mixer on medium speed, cream the butter and brown and granulated sugars together until light and fluffy.

3. Beat in the vanilla and egg. Scrape down the sides and bottom of the bowl with a spatula.

4. In a medium bowl, sift together the flour, baking powder, salt, cinnamon, and nutmeg. Add the dry ingredients and buttermilk to the butter-sugar mixture in the large bowl, alternating back and forth between the two, starting and ending with the flour mixture and beating on medium speed. Scrape down the sides and bottom of the bowl and stir in any unmixed bits of batter with a spatula. Fold in the peaches.

5. Pour the batter into the prepared skillet. Spread the batter out with a spatula. Bake until a toothpick inserted into the center comes out clean, 40 to 45 minutes.

6. Let it cool before slicing and serving from the pan.

STORAGE: Will keep tightly covered with plastic wrap or in an airtight container at room temperature for up to 2 days.

TOP IT OFF: If desired, add fresh, homemade Whipped Cream (page 130) to each slice before serving.

BLUEBERRY CORNMEAL SKILLET CAKE

This recipe is a new favorite. It's full of plump blueberries and sweet cornmeal. You can use fresh or frozen blueberries, so it's a great year-round skillet cake.

PREP TIME: 15 MINUTES • BAKE TIME: 45 MINUTES • YIELD: 8 SERVINGS

¾ cup buttermilk

½ cup (1 stick) unsalted butter, melted

1 teaspoon vanilla extract

2 large eggs, room temperature

1¼ cups all-purpose flour

1 cup granulated sugar

½ cup yellow cornmeal

2 teaspoons baking powder

½ teaspoon salt

2 cups fresh or frozen blueberries

1. Preheat the oven to 350°F. Coat a 10-inch skillet with nonstick baking spray with flour.

2. In a medium bowl, whisk the buttermilk, melted butter, vanilla, and eggs together until well combined.

3. In a large bowl, combine the flour, sugar, cornmeal, baking powder, and salt. Add in the buttermilk mixture and whisk together until the batter is smooth. Fold in the blueberries just until evenly distributed.

4. Pour the batter into the prepared skillet. Spread the batter out with a spatula. Bake until a toothpick inserted into the center comes out clean, 40 to 45 minutes.

5. Let it cool before slicing and serving from the pan.

STORAGE: Will keep tightly covered with plastic wrap or in an airtight container at room temperature for 3 to 4 days.

VARIATION: Substitute raspberries or blackberries for the blueberries, or add a little bit of each for a mixed berry cornmeal cake.

Funfetti Ramekin Cakes, page 118

LITTLE CAKES

If you're in need of some small-scale recipes, this chapter is for you. All of the recipes yield one or two small cakes. They're great if you're a family of two or if you simply have a serious craving for cake but don't need a cake that serves eight to twelve people.

Whatever you are craving, I have you covered—from flavorful bursts to go-to classic recipes such as chocolate and yellow cakes to a surprising and fun lime-and-coconut cake that is perfect for the summer months.

NUTELLA MUG CAKE

Chocolate and hazelnut make for a great mug cake
that's irresistible. Luckily, this moist cake is ready to eat in 2 minutes.
This is best enjoyed as soon as it is made.

PREP TIME: 3 MINUTES • BAKE TIME: 2 MINUTES • YIELD: 1 SERVING

2 tablespoons
salted butter

⅓ cup Nutella
chocolate-hazelnut
spread

1½ teaspoons
granulated sugar

¼ teaspoon
vanilla extract

¼ cup all-purpose flour

4 tablespoons whole
milk, divided

1. Microwave the butter in a large coffee cup for
   30 seconds.

2. Add the Nutella, sugar, and vanilla. Stir with a
   spoon until the Nutella is well combined. Add the
   flour and stir until it is completely worked into the
   batter. Add 2 tablespoons of the milk and stir until
   smooth. Add the remaining 2 tablespoons milk and
   stir until incorporated.

3. Microwave on high until there is no more batter
   sitting on the top of the cake, about 2 minutes. Let
   cool 1 to 2 minutes before serving.

VARIATION: You can switch out the Nutella for a plain
chocolate spread.

TOP IT OFF: Warm up 1 tablespoon of Nutella in the
microwave for 15 to 20 seconds and drizzle it on top
of the cake.

SNICKERDOODLE MUG CAKE

If you love snickerdoodle cookies, you will love this 2-minute mug cake.
It has cinnamon and sugar swirled throughout and sprinkled on top. Yum!
This is best enjoyed right after it is made.

PREP TIME: 3 MINUTES • BAKE TIME: 2 MINUTES • YIELD: 1 SERVING

2 tablespoons
salted butter

3 tablespoons
granulated
sugar, divided

¼ teaspoon
vanilla extract

5 tablespoons
all-purpose flour

¼ teaspoon cornstarch

¼ teaspoon
baking powder

4 tablespoons whole
milk, divided

½ teaspoon
ground cinnamon

1. Microwave the butter in a large coffee cup for 30 seconds.

2. Add 2 tablespoons of the sugar and the vanilla. Stir with a spoon until the sugar is worked into the butter. Add the flour, cornstarch, and baking powder, and stir until the flour is completely worked into the batter. Add 2 tablespoons of the milk and stir until smooth. Add the remaining 2 tablespoons of milk and stir until incorporated.

3. In a small bowl, combine the cinnamon and remaining 1 tablespoon sugar. Sprinkle three-quarters of the cinnamon-sugar mixture over the cake batter, then swirl it in with a skewer or butter knife. Sprinkle the remaining cinnamon-sugar mixture on top of the batter.

4. Microwave on high until there is no more batter sitting on the top of the cake, about 2 minutes. Let cool 1 to 2 minutes before serving.

TOP IT OFF: Take this dessert over the top with a scoop of vanilla ice cream.

CHOCOLATE MUG CAKE

This is a rich chocolate mug cake that will satisfy any chocolate craving. It's made with cocoa powder instead of baking chocolate and only takes 2 minutes to cook up. This is best enjoyed right after you make it.

PREP TIME: 3 MINUTES • BAKE TIME: 2 MINUTES • YIELD: 1 SERVING

2 tablespoons salted butter

3 tablespoons granulated sugar

¼ teaspoon vanilla extract

3 tablespoons all-purpose flour

1½ tablespoons unsweetened cocoa powder

¼ teaspoon baking powder

4 tablespoons whole milk, divided

1. Microwave the butter in a large coffee cup for 30 seconds.

2. Add the sugar and vanilla. Stir with a spoon until the sugar is worked into the butter. Add the flour, cocoa, and baking powder, and stir until the flour is completely worked into the batter. Add 2 tablespoons of the milk to the batter and stir until smooth. Add the remaining 2 tablespoons milk and stir until incorporated.

3. Microwave on high until there is no more batter sitting on the top of the cake, about 2 minutes. Let cool 1 to 2 minutes before serving.

TOP IT OFF: For an even more decadent experience, stir 1 to 2 tablespoons chocolate chips into the batter before cooking.

BANANA MUG CAKE

If you love banana bread, you will love this banana mug cake.
Use up the last ripe banana in this delicious recipe.
It's incredibly moist and flavored with ground cinnamon.
This is best enjoyed as soon as it is made.

PREP TIME: 3 MINUTES • BAKE TIME: 2 MINUTES • YIELD: 1 SERVING

2 tablespoons
salted butter

2 tablespoons packed
light brown sugar

¼ teaspoon
vanilla extract

⅓ cup mashed banana
(about 1 medium banana)

¼ cup all-purpose flour

¼ teaspoon
baking powder

¼ teaspoon
ground cinnamon

1 tablespoon whole milk

1. Microwave the butter in a large coffee cup for 30 seconds.

2. Add the brown sugar, vanilla, and banana. Stir with a spoon until the banana is worked into the batter. Add the flour, baking powder, and cinnamon, and stir until the flour is completely worked in.

3. Add the milk and stir until smooth.

4. Microwave on high until there is no more batter sitting on the top of the cake, about 2 minutes. Let cool 1 to 2 minutes before serving.

VARIATION: For a Banana Nut Mug Cake, add 1 to 2 tablespoons of chopped walnuts to the batter before cooking.

PEANUT BUTTER MUG CAKE

This is my go-to mug cake recipe. The cake is stuffed with peanut butter flavor. This is best enjoyed right away.

PREP TIME: 3 MINUTES • BAKE TIME: 2 MINUTES • YIELD: 1 SERVING

2 tablespoons
salted butter

¼ cup creamy
peanut butter

2 tablespoons packed
light brown sugar

¼ teaspoon
vanilla extract

¼ cup all-purpose flour

4 tablespoons whole
milk, divided

1. Microwave the butter in a large coffee cup for 30 seconds.

2. Add the peanut butter, brown sugar, and vanilla. Stir with a spoon until well combined. Add the flour and stir until the flour is completely worked into the batter. Add 2 tablespoons of the milk and stir until smooth. Add the remaining 2 tablespoons of milk and stir until incorporated.

3. Microwave on high until there is no more batter sitting on the top of the cake, about 2 minutes. Let cool 1 to 2 minutes before serving.

VARIATION: Instead of peanut butter, use the nut butter of your choice.

PEPPERMINT WHITE CHOCOLATE MUG CAKE

This cake is a cup of Christmas. It is spiked with peppermint flavor, with plenty of white chocolate chips throughout. Enjoy this right away.

PREP TIME: 3 MINUTES • BAKE TIME: 2 MINUTES • YIELD: 1 SERVING

2 tablespoons
salted butter

2 tablespoons
granulated sugar

¼ teaspoon
vanilla extract

¼ teaspoon
peppermint extract

¼ cup all-purpose flour

¼ teaspoon
baking powder

3 tablespoons whole
milk, divided

1½ tablespoons white
chocolate chips

1. Microwave the butter in a large coffee cup for 30 seconds.

2. Add the sugar, vanilla, and peppermint extract. Stir with a spoon until well combined. Add the flour and baking powder, and stir until the flour is completely worked into the batter. Add 2 tablespoons of the milk and stir until smooth. Add the remaining 1 tablespoon of milk and stir until incorporated. Sprinkle the chocolate chips on top and swirl them into the batter with a butter knife.

3. Microwave on high until there is no more batter sitting on the top of the cake, about 2 minutes. Let cool 1 to 2 minutes before serving.

TOP IT OFF: Max out the Christmas and decadence factors by topping with a scoop of vanilla ice cream and a crushed peppermint stick.

APPLE BUTTER SPICE MUG CAKE

Every fall should be kicked off with one of these! Loaded with apple butter and cinnamon, this cake is incredibly warm and comforting on a crisp autumn day. This is best enjoyed right away.

PREP TIME: 3 MINUTES ● BAKE TIME: 2 MINUTES 20 SECONDS ● YIELD: 1 SERVING

2 tablespoons
salted butter

¼ cup apple butter

2 tablespoons packed
light brown sugar

¼ teaspoon
vanilla extract

¼ cup all-purpose flour

¼ teaspoon
baking powder

¼ teaspoon
ground cinnamon

1 tablespoon whole milk

1. Microwave the butter in a large coffee cup for 30 seconds.

2. Add the apple butter, brown sugar, and vanilla. Stir with a spoon until well combined. Add the flour, baking powder, and cinnamon, and stir until the flour is completely worked into the batter.

3. Add the milk and stir until smooth.

4. Microwave on high until there is no more batter sitting on the top of the cake, 2 minutes 15 seconds to 2 minutes 20 seconds. Let cool 1 to 2 minutes before serving.

TOP IT OFF: If you're craving a topping, consider a little Cream Cheese Glaze (page 127). This mug cake also tastes delicious with a sprinkle of cinnamon sugar on top.

YELLOW CAKE FOR TWO

This is baked in a 6-inch round baking pan. It's the perfect size for two people or even a baby's smash cake. It's moist and fluffy, too.

PREP TIME: 10 MINUTES • BAKE TIME: 30 MINUTES • YIELD: 2 SERVINGS

½ cup granulated sugar

6 tablespoons (¾ stick) unsalted butter, at room temperature

1 teaspoon vanilla extract

1 large egg

¾ cup all-purpose flour

½ teaspoon baking powder

½ teaspoon baking soda

⅛ teaspoon salt

¼ cup buttermilk

1. Preheat the oven to 350°F. Coat a 6-inch round baking pan with nonstick baking spray with flour.

2. In a medium bowl, using an electric mixer on medium speed, cream the sugar and butter together until light and fluffy. Beat in the vanilla, then the egg, just until incorporated.

3. In a small bowl, combine the flour, baking powder, baking soda, and salt. Add the dry ingredients and buttermilk to the butter-sugar mixture in the medium bowl, alternating back and forth between the two, starting and ending with the flour mixture and beating on medium speed. Scrape down the sides and bottom of the bowl and stir in any unmixed bits of batter with a spatula.

4. Pour the batter into the prepared baking pan. Bake until a toothpick inserted into the center comes out clean, about 30 minutes.

5. Let cool for 5 minutes in the baking pan, then turn out onto a wire rack to cool completely.

STORAGE: Will keep tightly covered with plastic wrap or in an airtight container at room temperature for 4 to 5 days.

TOP IT OFF: Why not go with one of the birthday classics: Chocolate Frosting (page 125) or Vanilla Frosting (page 124)?

LIME-AND-COCONUT RAMEKIN CAKES

If you love a fruity cake, you will love these little guys, packed with lime and coconut flavors from bottled key lime juice and coconut extract. Both can be found in any large supermarket.

PREP TIME: 5 MINUTES • BAKE TIME: 35 MINUTES • YIELD: 2 SERVINGS

⅓ cup granulated sugar

¼ cup vegetable oil

1 teaspoon coconut extract

½ teaspoon vanilla extract

1 large egg

½ cup all-purpose flour

½ teaspoon baking powder

⅛ teaspoon salt

2½ tablespoons whole milk

1½ tablespoons key lime juice

1. Preheat the oven to 350°F. Coat two 6-ounce ramekins with nonstick baking spray with flour.

2. In a medium bowl, using an electric mixer on medium speed, beat the sugar and oil together until combined. Beat in the coconut extract and vanilla, then add the egg, beating just until incorporated.

3. In a small bowl, combine the flour, baking powder, and salt. In another small bowl, whisk together the milk and lime juice. Add the dry ingredients and the lime-milk mixture to the medium bowl, alternating back and forth between the two, starting and ending with the flour mixture and beating on medium speed. Scrape down the sides and bottom of the bowl and stir in any unmixed bits of batter with a spatula.

4. Pour the batter into the prepared ramekins. Place the ramekins on a baking sheet to prevent any batter from spilling into the oven. Bake until a tooth-pick inserted into the center comes out clean, 30 to 35 minutes.

5. Let cool for 5 minutes in the ramekins, then turn out onto a wire rack to cool completely.

STORAGE: Will keep tightly covered with plastic wrap or in an airtight container at room temperature for 4 to 5 days.

VARIATION: For a stronger coconut flavor, swap out the regular milk for coconut milk.

TOP IT OFF: These are delicious with a dollop of homemade Whipped Cream (page 130) with about 1 teaspoon grated lime zest added to it and a sprinkling of toasted shredded coconut.

FUNFETTI RAMEKIN CAKES

This is a yellow cake with sprinkles folded into the batter. It's a great cake to make when there are only two people to feed but a celebration to be had.

PREP TIME: 5 MINUTES • BAKE TIME: 30 MINUTES • YIELD: 2 SERVINGS

⅓ cup granulated sugar

¼ cup vegetable oil

½ teaspoon
vanilla extract

1 large egg

½ cup all-purpose flour

½ teaspoon
baking powder

⅛ teaspoon salt

¼ cup whole milk

1 tablespoon
multicolor sprinkles

1. Preheat the oven to 350°F. Coat two 6-ounce ramekins with nonstick baking spray with flour.

2. In a medium bowl, using an electric mixer on medium speed, beat the sugar and oil together until combined. Beat in the vanilla, then add the egg, beating just until incorporated.

3. In a small bowl, combine the flour, baking powder, and salt. Add the dry ingredients and milk to the sugar mixture in the medium bowl, alternating back and forth between the two, starting and ending with the flour mixture and beating on medium speed. Scrape down the sides and bottom of the bowl and stir in any unmixed bits of batter with a spatula. Fold the sprinkles into the batter until evenly distributed.

4. Pour the batter into the prepared ramekins. Place the ramekins on a baking sheet to prevent the batter from spilling into the oven. Bake until a toothpick inserted into the center comes out clean, 25 to 30 minutes.

5. Let cool for 5 minutes in the ramekins, then turn out onto a wire rack to cool completely.

STORAGE: Will keep tightly covered with plastic wrap or in an airtight container at room temperature for 4 to 5 days.

VARIATION: Switch out the multicolor sprinkles for candy-coated chocolate.

TRES LECHES RAMEKIN CAKES

This is so light and fluffy. The three different milks soaked in the cake make it a melt-in-your-mouth dessert.

PREP TIME: 7 MINUTES • BAKE TIME: 35 MINUTES, PLUS 1 HOUR TO CHILL • YIELD: 2 SERVINGS

FOR THE CAKE

1 large egg, separated

⅓ cup granulated sugar, plus 1 teaspoon, divided

1 teaspoon vanilla extract

2 tablespoons whole milk

¼ cup all-purpose flour

½ teaspoon baking powder

Pinch salt

FOR THE TOPPING

1 tablespoon evaporated milk

1 tablespoon sweetened condensed milk

½ tablespoon whole milk

1. Preheat the oven to 350°F. Coat two 6-ounce ramekins with nonstick baking spray with flour.

2. For the cake, in a small bowl, using an electric mixer on medium speed, beat the egg white until foamy.

3. In a medium bowl, beat the egg yolk and ⅓ cup of sugar together, until the mixture is pale yellow. Add the vanilla and milk, and gently stir to combine. Add the remaining 1 teaspoon of sugar. Continue to beat the egg white until soft peaks form. Set aside.

4. Combine the flour, baking powder, and salt. Pour the dry ingredients into the yolk mixture and gently stir, just until the flour is incorporated. Using a spatula, fold in the beaten egg white, just until there are no more white streaks in the batter.

5. Pour the batter evenly into the two ramekins. Place the ramekins on a baking sheet to prevent spillage. Bake until a toothpick inserted into the center comes out clean, 30 to 35 minutes. Let the cakes cool completely before adding the topping.

6. For the topping, in a small bowl, whisk together the three milks. Pour it evenly over the tops of the two cooled cakes. Refrigerate the cakes for at least 1 hour (but preferably overnight) before serving in the ramekins.

STORAGE: Will keep tightly covered with plastic wrap or in an airtight container in the refrigerator for 2 to 3 days.

COOKIE DOUGH LAVA CAKES

This is always a hit and is best served hot. It's got a cookie dough texture with lots of melty chocolate chips.

PREP TIME: 10 MINUTES • BAKE TIME: 30 MINUTES • YIELD: 2 SERVINGS

FOR THE FILLING

2 tablespoons packed light brown sugar

1 tablespoon unsalted butter, at room temperature

½ tablespoon whole milk

¼ teaspoon vanilla extract

2½ tablespoons all-purpose flour

1 tablespoon milk chocolate chips

FOR THE CAKE

¼ cup packed light brown sugar

1½ tablespoons granulated sugar

2 tablespoons unsalted butter, at room temperature

1 teaspoon vanilla extract

1. Preheat the oven to 350°F. Coat two 6-ounce ramekins with nonstick baking spray with flour.

2. To make the filling, in a small bowl, using an electric mixer on medium speed, cream the brown sugar and butter together until combined. Beat in the milk and vanilla. Beat in the flour on medium speed until the flour is worked into the batter. Stir in the chocolate chips. Set aside.

3. To make the cake, in a medium bowl, using the mixer on medium speed, cream the brown and granulated sugars and butter together until light and fluffy. Beat in the vanilla, then add the egg, beating just until incorporated.

4. In another small bowl, combine the flour, baking powder, and salt.

5. Add the dry ingredients to the butter-sugar mixture in the medium bowl and beat on medium speed, just until the flour is worked in. Stir in the chocolate chips.

1 large egg

½ cup all-purpose flour

½ teaspoon
baking powder

Pinch salt

2 tablespoons milk
chocolate chips

6. Pour half of the batter evenly into the two prepared ramekins. Divide the cookie dough filling and place half in the center of each ramekin on top of the batter. Cover the filling with the remaining batter. Place the ramekins on a baking sheet to prevent the batter from spilling into the oven. Bake until a toothpick inserted into the center comes out clean, about 30 minutes.

7. Let cool for 5 minutes in the baking pan and serve hot.

VARIATION: Substitute any kind of baking chip you like for the chocolate chips.

Clockwise: Whipped Cream, page 130;
Vanilla Frosting, page 124; Chocolate Ganache, page 126

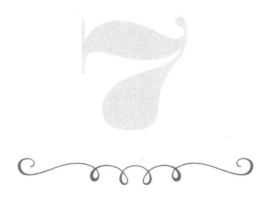

TOPPINGS

It's always nice to have a variety of basic toppings to use on your cakes. These are recipes that will become your go-tos when you need to whip up a frosting. The recipes have so few ingredients—often pantry staples—that it's easy to whip them up quickly and at a moment's notice.

I wanted a variety of toppings for this chapter. For that reason, I went with the two basic frosting recipes, a ganache, three glazes, and a homemade whipped cream. Each recipe can be used for the many different cakes included in the book.

VANILLA FROSTING

This is the classic American vanilla frosting. It's quick to whip up, has basic ingredients, and is perfectly sweetened.

PREP TIME: 5 MINUTES • YIELD: 3½ CUPS

1 cup (2 sticks) unsalted butter, at room temperature

3½ tablespoons whole milk

2 teaspoons vanilla extract

¼ teaspoon salt

3½ cups powdered sugar, divided

1. In a large bowl, using an electric mixer on medium speed, beat the butter until creamy. Beat in the milk, vanilla, and salt. On low speed, beat in 1¾ cups of the powdered sugar until most of the powdered sugar is worked into the mixture. Add in the remaining 1¾ cups of powdered sugar and continue to beat on low speed until it is incorporated.

2. Turn the mixer on high speed and beat for an additional 30 seconds, until the frosting is light and fluffy.

STORAGE: If not using right away, gently press plastic wrap directly on top of the frosting to prevent a crust from forming and store at room temperature for 2 to 3 days.

CHOCOLATE FROSTING

This is rich, creamy, and delicious. It uses cocoa powder instead of baking chocolate, which is always a pantry staple for me.

PREP TIME: 5 MINUTES • YIELD: 3½ CUPS

1 cup (2 sticks) unsalted butter, at room temperature

½ cup unsweetened cocoa powder

¼ cup whole milk

1 teaspoon vanilla extract

¼ teaspoon salt

3 cups powdered sugar, divided

1. In a large bowl, using an electric mixer on medium speed, beat the butter until creamy. Beat in the cocoa, milk, vanilla, and salt. Add 1½ cups of the powdered sugar, beating on low speed until most of the sugar is worked into the mixture. Add in the remaining 1½ cups of sugar and beat on low speed until incorporated.

2. Turn the mixer on high speed and beat for an additional 30 seconds, until the frosting is light and fluffy.

STORAGE: If not ready to use right away, gently press plastic wrap directly on top of the frosting to prevent a crust from forming and store at room temperature for 2 to 3 days.

CHOCOLATE GANACHE

Creamy and chocolatey, chocolate ganache can have a pourable
consistency (great for glazing) or a spreadable consistency.
The best part is that it only has two ingredients.

PREP TIME: 5 MINUTES • YIELD: 1½ CUPS

1 cup chocolate chips
(milk, semisweet,
bittersweet—your
choice)

½ cup heavy cream

1. In a medium microwave-safe bowl, microwave the
   chocolate chips and cream in 30-second intervals,
   stirring after each. Continue microwaving until the
   ganache is thick and smooth.

2. Use right away to drizzle over a cake or let it set
   up at room temperature for several hours until
   it's spreadable.

STORAGE: If not using right away, will keep covered with plastic wrap in the refrigerator for up to 2 days.

CHOCOLATE PEANUT BUTTER GANACHE: Follow the directions using ½ cup semisweet chocolate chips, ½ cup peanut butter chips, and ½ cup heavy cream.

MINT CHOCOLATE GANACHE: Follow the directions using 1 cup semisweet chocolate chips and ½ cup heavy cream. When the ganache is thick and smooth, stir in ¼ teaspoon mint extract.

MEXICAN CHOCOLATE GANACHE: Follow the directions using 1 cup semisweet chocolate chips and ½ cup heavy cream. When the ganache is thick and smooth, stir in ¼ teaspoon ground cinnamon and ¼ teaspoon cayenne pepper.

WHITE CHOCOLATE GANACHE: Follow the directions, but swap out the chocolate chips for white chocolate chips.

CREAM CHEESE GLAZE

This is a perfect topping for all of the coffee cake recipes.

PREP TIME: 5 MINUTES • YIELD: ¾ CUP

4 ounces cream cheese, at room temperature

1 cup powdered sugar

¼ cup whole milk

1 teaspoon vanilla extract

1. In a large bowl, using an electric mixer on medium speed, beat the cream cheese and powdered sugar together until fully combined. Scrape down the sides and bottom of the bowl.

2. Add the milk and vanilla and beat on low speed until the milk is worked into the glaze.

3. Drizzle the glaze on top of the cake.

STORAGE: If not using right away, will keep covered with plastic wrap in the refrigerator for 2 to 3 days.

VANILLA GLAZE

This is a great little topping for any cake. It's simple and adds a nice amount of sweetness to finish the dessert. It would be great for the Bundt or skillet cakes.

PREP TIME: 2 MINUTES • YIELD: ¾ CUP

1 cup powdered sugar

3 tablespoons heavy cream

1 teaspoon vanilla extract

1. In a medium bowl, whisk the powdered sugar, cream, and vanilla together until smooth.

2. Drizzle the glaze on top of the cake.

STORAGE: If not using right away, will keep covered with plastic wrap in the refrigerator for 6 to 7 days.

ORANGE GLAZE: Follow the directions using ¾ cup powdered sugar, 2 tablespoons orange juice, and the grated zest of 1 orange.

COFFEE GLAZE: Follow the directions using 1 cup powdered sugar and 1½ tablespoons strongly brewed coffee.

LEMON GLAZE: Follow the directions using ¾ cup powdered sugar, 2 tablespoons fresh lemon juice, and the grated zest of 1 lemon.

MARASCHINO CHERRY GLAZE: Follow the directions using ¾ cup powdered sugar and 2 tablespoons juice from a jar of maraschino cherries.

MAPLE GLAZE: Follow the directions using 1 cup powdered sugar, 3 tablespoons heavy cream, and 1 teaspoon maple extract.

PEANUT BUTTER GLAZE

This pairs particularly well with any cake that has chocolate in it.

PREP TIME: 5 MINUTES • YIELD: 1 CUP

¼ cup creamy
peanut butter

2 tablespoons
unsalted butter

6 tablespoons
whole milk

¼ teaspoon
vanilla extract

1¼ cups powdered
sugar

1. In a medium microwave-safe bowl, microwave the peanut butter and butter until melted, about 30 seconds. Whisk until smooth. Whisk in the milk and vanilla, then add the powdered sugar and whisk until smooth.

2. Drizzle the glaze on top of the cake.

STORAGE: If not using right away, this glaze will keep covered with plastic wrap in the refrigerator for 6 to 7 days.

WHIPPED CREAM

Whipped cream is always best when it's homemade. It's so simple to whip up with an electric mixer and tastes amazing.

PREP TIME: 5 MINUTES • YIELD: 2 CUPS

1 cup heavy cream

2 to 3 tablespoons powdered sugar

½ teaspoon vanilla extract

In a large bowl, using an electric mixer on medium speed, beat the cream, powdered sugar, and vanilla together until stiff peaks form.

STORAGE: If not using right away, immediately cover with plastic wrap and refrigerate for up to 3 days.

Measurement Conversions

OVEN TEMPERATURES

Fahrenheit	Celsius (approximate)
250°F	120°C
300°F	150°C
325°F	165°C
350°F	180°C
375°F	190°C
400°F	200°C
425°F	220°C
450°F	230°C

WEIGHT EQUIVALENTS

US Standard	Metric (approximate)
½ ounce	15 g
1 ounce	30 g
2 ounces	60 g
4 ounces	115 g
8 ounces	225 g
12 ounces	340 g
16 ounces or 1 pound	455 g

VOLUME EQUIVALENTS (LIQUID)

US Standard	US Standard (ounces)	Metric (approximate)
2 tablespoons	1 fl. oz.	30 mL
¼ cup	2 fl. oz.	60 mL
½ cup	4 fl. oz.	120 mL
1 cup	8 fl. oz.	240 mL
1½ cups	12 fl. oz.	355 mL
2 cups or 1 pint	16 fl. oz.	475 mL
4 cups or 1 quart	32 fl. oz.	1 L
1 gallon	128 fl. oz.	4 L

VOLUME EQUIVALENTS (DRY)

US Standard	Metric (approximate)
⅛ teaspoon	0.5 mL
¼ teaspoon	1 mL
½ teaspoon	2 mL
¾ teaspoon	4 mL
1 teaspoon	5 mL
1 tablespoon	15 mL
¼ cup	59 mL
⅓ cup	79 mL
½ cup	118 mL
⅔ cup	156 mL
¾ cup	177 mL
1 cup	235 mL
2 cups or 1 pint	475 mL
3 cups	700 mL
4 cups or 1 quart	1 L

Index

About the Author

Miranda Couse is a baker, photographer, and the creator behind the popular dessert blog Cookie Dough and Oven Mitt. Miranda is a lifelong baker and her recipes range from family favorites to innovative (and delicious) interpretations of popular classics. Her work has appeared in *Redbook, Country Living,* and *Parade* magazines and Buzzfeed. She bakes for her son and husband in upstate New York.

CPSIA information can be obtained
at www.ICGtesting.com
Printed in the USA
BVHW091457090520
579380BV00014B/702